WITHDRAWN

Folio
HV
699
.A62
92

Y0-DCH-290

HELPING CHILDREN BY STRENGTHENING FAMILIES

A LOOK AT FAMILY SUPPORT PROGRAMS

by MaryLee Allen, Patricia Brown, and Belva Finlay

Children's Defense Fund

HIEBERT LIBRARY   37062
Fresno Pacific College - M.B. Seminary
Fresno, CA 93702

Copyright © 1992 Children's Defense Fund
ISBN: 0-938008-94-3

Library of Congress Catalog
Card No: 92-073171

Children's Defense Fund
25 E Street, N.W.
Washington, DC 20001

Notes on language. For consistency, CDF uniformly uses the terms black and Latino, recognizing that some people prefer the alternatives, African American and Hispanic.

Acknowledgments

CDF owes special thanks to the staff members of the many wonderful family support programs featured in this book, many of whom talked with us at length about the development and operation of their programs. They helped us understand what makes them work and introduced us to the families and children they serve. We are grateful for the information they shared and the hospitality they showed us on site visits. Most of all we admire their strong commitment to supporting families.

We also are grateful to Bernice Weissbourd and Heather Weiss, whose pioneering and continuing work in the area of family support has paved the way for others. Mildred Winter, Rosalie Streett, Judy Carter, Carol Williams, and Frank Farrow also helped us better understand the essential characteristics of strong family support programs. We thank them and the many others who have studied and written about these programs for their thoughtful reflections and for the time and energy they have devoted to strengthening the family support movement.

Much of CDF's work to date to support efforts to strengthen and preserve families has been funded through the generous support of the Edna McConnell Clark Foundation. That work on behalf of families in crisis has contributed to our commitment to ensuring earlier support to families, before problems intensify. The preparation and printing of this book was financed in part through the support of Kraft General Foods. The Charles H. Revson Foundation provides support for all CDF publications.

Finally, we want to thank CDF staff members whose hard work made this book a reality. Olivia Golden offered encouragement and thoughtful advice. Joanne Butler not only typed and retyped, but kept all of us organized, as well. David Heffernan, Donna M. Jablonski, Janis Johnston, and Deneice Patterson did the editing and production.

Contents

III

Putting Family Support Principles to Work 69

About This Report

The Children's Defense Fund (CDF) is publishing this book on family support and parent education programs for three reasons:

- We want every child to get the best possible start in life.
- We believe in preventing problems before they become serious and require costly treatment.
- We believe that all parents must be prepared for and supported in their parenting role, so they will be able to do the best possible job of nurturing and protecting their children. Parents and family are fundamental to their children's early and later development and hold the keys to their children's future.

By strengthening families' ability to nurture their children physically, emotionally, and intellectually, family support programs increase the likelihood that children will grow up healthy, safe, and successful. By focusing on early and comprehensive support for parents, these programs ensure the best prevention of all: They enable parents to respond early to their children's multiple needs, within the family, and before healthy development is compromised. By giving parents information early on about the way young children learn and develop, these programs make it far more likely that parents will support their children's healthy development and enhance their children's later school performance.

Family support and parent education programs currently are improving the lives of thousands of families and children. Yet many policy makers, advocates, and service providers who traditionally have focused on children are unfamiliar with these efforts or are unsure of what it is these programs do or how they fit into the broad array of services to help children.

This report provides child advocates and others who work for children's well-being a clearer idea of what family support programs do, how they operate, and why they are effective—not just for low-income families or families with serious problems, but for all families. Family support programs are an important complement to—but in no way a substitute for—such basic family supports as adequate income; decent housing, health care, and child care; and good schools. Family support programs also complement, but are different from, family and medical leave and other policies that can help parents better carry out their parenting responsibilities.

We hope this report also spurs child advocates, community leaders, and policy makers at all levels to foster the development of family support programs in communities across the country. This is an agenda we need to move forward immediately, for every day it becomes more apparent that all parents, at one time or another, need some kind of help.

But our family support agenda cannot stop there. The principles of family support must become part of the delivery of *all* services for children and their families—ranging from education to health care to child protection services. Specific program examples in this report show how providers of services for children and families, with support from advocates and policy makers, can take concrete steps to make their existing programs more responsive to families and therefore more effective for children.

The report is divided into three parts. The first lays out the basic principles of family support, traces its historical and disciplinary roots, and contrasts the family support approach with traditional social services. The section suggests CDF's answers to such questions as, "Why do we need family support services?" and "Which families need them?"

In the second part we describe a variety of family support and parent education programs in action, along with other types of programs that have added a family support or parent education component. We deliberately selected a wide variety of programs serving diverse families to demonstrate the broad applicability of family support principles. In this section we also briefly review some of the research demonstrating the positive impact of parent education and family support activities on children and parents.

Drawing on the experience of the programs described in the second section and on the observations of other family support experts, the final section examines the challenges involved in establishing successful and lasting family support programs. We also discuss briefly the importance of incorporating family support principles into other human service systems. Finally, we conclude with CDF's specific recommendations for steps that must be taken at the federal, state, and community levels to implement community-based family support programs that will help parents nurture and protect their children.

"If a community values its children,
it must cherish their parents."

John Bowlby, *Child Care and the Growth of Love*

What Are Family Support Programs?

magine a place...
   ...where a young mother can go for support and encouragement when she feels overwhelmed by her responsibilities at home.
   ...where she and her children can drop in for a hot lunch, visit with other mothers while the children play, and get some professional advice about a child's special health care needs.
   ...where someone has the time to sit and talk with her about her own education goals and help her plan the next step toward reaching them.
   ...where a group of parents can sit and talk with a professional about how to help their children cope with violence in their neighborhood.
   ...where a parent who has just completed a drug treatment program or had her children returned from foster care can go to find out about available community resources.

Imagine a place...
   ...that sends someone to accompany a pregnant teenager to a health clinic for her first prenatal visit if she is nervous about going alone.
   ...that sends a home visitor to a young mother's apartment to talk about childrearing, show her how to stimulate her child's development, and connect her with the special services her child may need.
   ...that a young mother can call for advice and support when she is having trouble with her children and doesn't know what to do next.

   Imagine a place where caring staff members recognize how difficult it is to raise children and praise parents for their efforts.

   Such places exist. They are most often called family support centers or family resource centers, and sometimes, parent education programs. In the past decade or so they have sprouted up in communities across the country.
   Some of these places have catchy names such as Kids Place, Bananas, and Learning Tree. Others have more formal names: Early Childhood and Family Education Program. Some are drop-in centers located in renovated houses in neighborhoods. Some have offices located in schools or office buildings and send home visitors into the community to visit families. Some aren't really "places" at all, but rely solely on home visitors to bring information and support to families in their homes on a regular basis. Some family

support efforts are single programs; others are part of a network of similar programs.

Despite outward differences, all family support programs work toward the same basic goal of strengthening families to ensure the well-being and healthy development of the next generation. They do this by:

- Helping parents cope with the stresses of daily life.
- Giving parents new information and ideas about child development and childrearing to make parenting more rewarding and help them nurture and support their children better.
- Reducing the isolation many parents feel by bringing them into contact with other parents in similar circumstances.
- Linking families with other social services and supports that can help meet their basic needs, ideally before the needs intensify and reach crisis proportions.

Why Do We Need Family Support Programs?

Raising children to be self-confident, responsible citizens who can achieve their full potential always has been one of the most challenging and demanding jobs any adult can undertake. And in many ways it is even harder now than it used to be. Once, extended families were likely to be available for advice, babysitting, an emergency loan, and a shared meal. Family doctors, ministers, and rabbis offered parents help with their questions about childrearing. Now, many parents are isolated, without strong ties to their neighborhood and with few kin to call on. With the recent increases in divorce rates and

How Family Support Differs from Traditional Services

Family Support Services	Traditional Services
Help to prevent crises by meeting needs early	Intervene after crises occur and needs intensify
Offer help meeting basic needs, special services, and referrals	Offer only specific services or treatments
Respond flexibly to family and community needs	Program and funding source dictate services
Focus on families	Focus on individuals
Build on family strengths	Emphasize family deficits
Reach out to families	Have strict eligibility requirements
Often offer drop-in services	Have rigid office hours
Respond quickly to needs	Often have waiting lists
Offer services in family's home or in home-like centers	Services are office-based

rates of births to unmarried women, more and more women are raising their children without a partner, which makes a difficult job even harder.

Young families headed by persons younger than 30—in which most children spend their youngest and most developmentally vulnerable years—have been particularly hard hit in the past two decades by a cycle of falling incomes, increasing family disintegration, and rising poverty. According to a report published in 1992 by the Children's Defense Fund, *Vanishing Dreams: The Economic Plight of America's Young Families,* the median annual income of young families with children dropped 32 percent from 1973 to 1990, after adjusting for inflation. The damage has cut so broadly and deeply that now one in four white children in young families, one in five children in married-couple young families, and one in three children in families headed by young high school graduates are poor. For minority children these trends have been most devastating. The median earnings of the heads of young black families with children fell 71 percent; two out of three children in young black families now are poor.

Young families not only lost income, but as the permanence and quality of their jobs

A CASE STUDY

Family Support Helps Families Cope with Difficult Times

Isabel first came to the Family Place (see page 22), a drop-in family support center, when her baby son was nine months old and her daughters were seven and nine. She had just left her husband, who was abusive when he drank, and was staying with her children at her mother-in-law's apartment. She was frightened and confused and needed someone with whom she could talk.

At the Family Place Isabel was assigned a social worker to help her decide what she wanted to do next. Isabel also made friends with other neighborhood mothers who came to the center. Her young son was screened to make sure he had no physical or developmental problems, and she began attending some of the parenting classes and support groups held there. At a Family Place Red Cross sewing class, she rediscovered her love of sewing and eventually began to teach the class. She also became one of the leaders in organizing a sewing co-op.

Isabel decided she wanted to return to her husband, and soon she became pregnant. Still unhappy with her husband's behavior and discouraged by the prospect of another child to care for, Isabel relied heavily on her Family Place social worker and another Family Place mother, called a First Friend, for extra emotional support during her pregnancy. They made sure she went for regular prenatal checkups and attended the special prenatal care and exercise class at the Family Place. After her healthy baby son was born, Isabel began providing day care for several other infants who were children of Family Place participants.

Isabel and her children no longer receive direct services from Family Place, but Isabel phones and drops in frequently. Recently she asked for advice on how to react to her landlord's threats to evict her and other families from her building. Family Place referred her to a nonprofit housing counseling service, which was able to help.

deteriorated, they also frequently lost fringe benefits such as health insurance. Falling incomes also have hurt young families in an increasingly expensive housing market. One-third fewer young families with children were homeowners in 1991 than in 1980. High rents are forcing more and more families to double up, and many eventually become homeless. A shrinking proportion of families can afford to give their children extras such as music lessons or summer vacations. Parents face a continuous struggle to balance the demands of family life and the jobs necessary to make ends meet. As a result many children and parents spend little time together.

While the economic challenges are getting tougher, the public safety net that used to provide the basics for poor families has developed gaping holes. Help in the form of unemployment insurance benefits, Aid to Families with Dependent Children (AFDC), food stamps, the Special Supplemental Food Program for Women, Infants, and Children (WIC), Medicaid coverage, and low-cost health care at community clinics has failed to keep up with increased need. Government programs were less than half as effective in pulling young families out of poverty in 1990 as they were in 1979.

In addition, many families today are exposed to dangers almost unknown a generation ago. In some neighborhoods, parents can't allow their children to play outside—even in front of their own homes—for fear of violence. Sometimes parents can't even be sure their children will be safe inside. And in all neighborhoods parents are feeling uncertain about how to teach their children strong values and how to help them succeed in school and resist negative peer pressure.

Parents used to be able to depend to some degree on society to reinforce the values they taught at home—the importance of study, hard work, and non-material rewards, for example, or concern for others, responsibility, and respect for authority. Today a barrage of messages from the mass culture promotes and glamorizes the opposite values, meaning that parents constantly struggle against the tide to teach their values to their children.

What Are the Basic Principles of Family Support?

In general, family support programs offer some of the help that used to come from kin and community. They aim to keep families healthy and intact through a broad range of preventive and supportive services delivered with flexibility, personalized attention, and cultural sensitivity.

The fundamental principles of family support have been identified and discussed extensively by Bernice Weissbourd, a long-time leader of the family support movement, and Heather Weiss, director of the Harvard Family Research Project, among others. The following summary draws heavily on their work.

Family support programs:

• *Emphasize the family unit.* For parents and children, the avenues to rewarding, successful lives are intertwined. Family support programs offer parents help and encouragement in meeting the demands of work and family life so they, in turn, can do a better job of nurturing their children.

• *Build on family strengths.* All parents want to do their best for their children, and this desire is a powerful motivator for change. Family support programs are based on the truth that every parent has skills and talents that can be developed to improve family functioning.

America's Families Under Stress

Declining Family Income

- Between 1973 and 1990, the median income of young families with children (those headed by someone younger than 30) plunged by nearly one-third—32 percent—after adjusting for inflation.
- Forty percent of all children in young families were living in poverty in 1990.
- Full-time, year-round work at the minimum wage of $4.25 an hour gives a family of three an income that equals only 80 percent of the 1991 poverty level.

More Births to Teens

- In 1989 there were 517,989 births to women younger than 20. Roughly two-thirds of these births were to unmarried teenagers, and about one-quarter of the total were repeat births.
- The 1989 teen birth rate of 58.1 births per 1,000 teenagers was the highest teen birth rate since 1970.

Lack of Access to Health Care

- Forty percent of all children lacked employer health coverage in 1990, even though more than 85 percent of all children lived in working families. The gaps in Medicaid and private insurance left 8.4 million children with no health insurance at all.
- In 1989 only about one-quarter of all infants were born to mothers who received early prenatal care, the lowest proportion since 1978. The proportion of infants born to mothers who received late or no prenatal care (6.4 percent) was higher than in any year since 1973.
- In nine major cities, only 10 to 42 percent of children starting school in 1991 had received appropriate preschool vaccinations on time.

Growing Hunger and Homelessness

- About 5.5 million children younger than 12 (one in eight) don't regularly get enough to eat.
- An estimated 100,000 children go to sleep homeless each night.

More Children and Families in Crisis

- More than 4.5 million women of childbearing age were current users of illegal drugs in 1990.
- At the peak of the crack crisis, as many as 375,000 infants were estimated to be born drug-exposed each year.
- An estimated 2.7 million children were reported abused or neglected in 1991, up from 1.1 million in 1980. Neglect cases accounted for about half of all reports.
- In 1990 an estimated 407,000 children were in foster care, an increase of almost 50 percent since 1986. Infants comprise a growing percentage of children entering care in some states.

A CASE STUDY

Family Support Programs Stress Prevention

Ricky was a quiet 14-month-old who relied on his body for communication. Some of his behaviors, such as pointing and gesturing, were appropriate; others, such as biting and hitting, were worrisome. His mother, Sandra, had been abused as a child by her mother, and Sandra was afraid of repeating this pattern when she became frustrated with Ricky.

A WIC nurse, who was also concerned about his walking, suggested that Ricky be evaluated by the CEDEN Parent-Child Program, a home-visitor family support program in Austin, Texas (see page 28). CEDEN's assessment showed no gross motor development problems, but Ricky's language development was delayed significantly. A home visitor began working with the family. When Ricky's first quarterly assessment showed continued language delay, a CEDEN speech pathologist began to accompany the home visitor on her weekly visits. The speech pathologist showed Sandra how to communicate with Ricky in certain ways that would help his language development and urged her to increase his contact with other children.

Sandra had expressed a desire to find a job, and the home visitor encouraged her to begin doing volunteer work and, later, to enroll in a job training program that provides child care through the Texas Employment Commission. Sandra now participates in the program about 20 hours a week. Meanwhile, Ricky's language has shown great improvement.

The CEDEN home visitor continues to visit every week to help Ricky and Sandra sustain their progress.

• *Make participation voluntary.* Coercion wins few hearts. People who initiate change generally are willing to work harder at it than those who are forced to change. Moreover, if support services are available that truly meet families' needs, the issue of coercion becomes moot.

• *Address family needs comprehensively.* Many families have multiple, interrelated needs. When a broad range of services are offered in a coordinated fashion, a parent and case manager can develop a multi-prong attack on the family's problems, in which the pieces reinforce each other. For example, many parents first get enthusiastic about finishing their own education when they begin to get involved in helping their preschool children get ready for school. If a mother can study for her General Educational Development degree (GED) in the building where her four-year-old attends preschool and she attends a parent education class, the chances of her completing her GED are greatly increased. When she then is helped to find a job and is able to better support her child, both have improved chances for success.

• *Develop parenting skills.* Many young parents have had little experience with infants and young children; others didn't get enough affection or attention as young children themselves. Parents with children who have disabilities frequently need extra help in meeting their children's special needs. When family support programs provide parents with information about child development, nutrition, discipline, or their children's special treatment needs, their self-confidence and effectiveness as parents blossom.

• *Provide nurturing connections with others.* Many young parents feel lonely and isolated. Family support programs offer them opportunities to make friends with others in similar circumstances, share their struggles and their successes, and gain strength from each other. Family support programs are careful to employ only highly empathetic professionals and paraprofessionals who treat families with respect and whose goal is to empower families to take control of their lives. In many programs, graduates become paraprofessional staff members.

• *Respond to individual and community needs.* Through strong case management and careful program design, family support programs tailor their efforts to meet the individual needs of those they serve. In communities where alcohol abuse or family violence is prevalent, for example, special programs address those problems. When lack of public transportation is a problem, centers often provide rides to medical appointments and other activities. In many family support programs, home visitors give families highly personalized attention.

• *Work to prevent crises.* Since prevention is always more effective than remediation, many family support programs seek to begin strengthening the parent-child bond as early as possible—even through parenting education programs before an infant is born. After a birth, staff members help parents adjust to the demands of a new baby, and later they offer help in solving family problems *before* crises such as school failure, family violence, severe medical problems, or homelessness have a chance to develop.

• *Respect individual and cultural differences.* Strengthening families doesn't mean molding them into one form. Family support programs work hard to preserve and enhance the cultural identities of participating families. Programs that serve minority communities generally try to employ staff members who come from the community and speak the language likely to be spoken in the homes.

• *Coordinate and cooperate with other agencies.* In every community there are many existing public and private agencies that offer valuable services to families. The challenge is to overcome the bureaucratic hurdles, coordinate the services, and make them respon-

How the U.S. Measures Up in Supporting Families

	Health insurance for all children?	Family allowance for all families with children?	Paid parental leave?
Austria	Yes	Yes	Yes
Canada	Yes	Yes	Yes
France	Yes	Yes	Yes
Germany	Yes	Yes	Yes
Sweden	Yes	Yes	Yes
United Kingdom	Yes	Yes	Yes
United States	**No**	**No**	**No**

sive to community needs. Family support programs act as brokers between the families they serve and existing services, while identifying and filling in the service gaps to create a continuous web of family supports.

Family support programs cannot solve all the problems that plague families. They cannot replace income or housing assistance, for example, or job training and job placement programs, or good-quality child care or health care. These basic supports should be available to every family in a wealthy democracy such as the United States.

Neither can family support programs, by themselves, rescue all deeply troubled families. Some families need more intensive help than family support programs can offer, and some children may need to receive help away from their families. Even if there were a family support program in every neighborhood, special programs still would be needed for families in which children are endangered. Some families still would need comprehensive drug and alcohol treatment programs and therapeutic community-based programs for children with serious emotional problems. But the number of children and families needing such intensive help almost certainly would be reduced.

Although family support programs cannot be substitutes for other services, they are an ideal source of ongoing support for families that are recovering from a serious crisis and need help to sustain their progress. Such families include those that have completed an intensive family preservation program because a child was at imminent risk of placement in foster care (see page 72), families that are being reunited with children temporarily placed in foster care, families recovering from drug or alcohol abuse, and families trying to reestablish a normal family life after a period of homelessness.

A CASE STUDY

Family Support Gives School-Age Children a Boost

Nine-year-old David was having a hard time keeping up academically with his class when the Waverly Family Center's Youth Coordinator first interested him in coming to the center's after-school program (see page 46). After David and a volunteer tutor began working together once a week, it became apparent that communication and coordination between home, school, and the tutoring program was needed. So David's tutor, a graduate student in education, visited both David's mother and his teacher to talk about his difficulties with his studies. The three of them worked out a coordinated strategy to help David improve his school performance.

David is now 11. He has been coming to Waverly Center regularly for two years. His grades have improved and he is keeping up with his class. In addition to receiving tutoring, he participates in other Waverly activities for school-age children, including a summer day camp in the neighborhood. As a member of Waverly's Teen Club for 11- to 13-year-olds, David goes on field trips twice a month. The club also meets every week at the center. Recently during a club meeting, members wrote "Dear Abby" letters about problems at home or at school that were bothering them. Then the group discussed solutions to each problem.

David says he likes coming to the center to do interesting things with his friends, and he credits the tutoring program for the strides he is making in school.

Which Families Need Support?

In today's complex world no family has within itself all of the knowledge and resources necessary to meet all of its members' needs. Parents in different circumstances need different kinds of help and different levels of support, but all parents need some kind of help at one time or another.

A recent evaluation of Parents as Teachers, the statewide parent education program in Missouri, brings this message home. The researchers found that even among participating two-parent, non-minority families with mothers having at least a high school education—families not traditionally considered at risk—there were many indications that all was not well for healthy child development. Almost half of these families showed family stress and poor coping skills, poor parent-child communication, and delays in their children's development.

Some middle-class families don't realize they receive help in raising their families; they think "help" is the assistance provided by public agencies to poor families. They don't recognize as "help" the various forms of assistance that generally are available or can be purchased in middle-class neighborhoods: prenatal exercise classes at a local gym, paid babysitters and child care, parenting classes at the local YWCA, books on child development, private family counseling, visits to a private pediatrician, and the assistance available to all members of a community through religious organizations, schools, libraries, and community centers.

Although many middle-income families may not need financial help to pay for basic services such as child care or health insurance coverage, they often can benefit from the peer support that a family support program offers. And they are likely to benefit from a better understanding of child development and help in developing their parenting skills, particularly if they are young or are coping with stressful family events.

Lower income families have similar needs, but they also may need help obtaining child care, health care, housing assistance, or employment. Because these parents may be overwhelmed by the pressures of poverty, they also may need special assistance in coping with the daily demands of childrearing. Family support staff members also can help these parents set goals for themselves and get the assistance they need to succeed.

For very young parents, raising children can be especially difficult. They typically have less money and fewer personal resources and skills to draw on in solving family problems than older parents do. Teen parents' own needs for self-discovery and independence may conflict with their parental responsibilities. Family support programs help young parents recognize and understand these conflicts, offering them opportunities to continue their own personal and educational development while learning how to become responsible parents.

Because children develop so rapidly during their first years, and because early development is so critical to later success in school and life, most family support programs tend to target their primary efforts to parents of young children. The programs help parents keep abreast of their infants' and toddlers' changing needs and adapt their own behavior and expectations to ensure their children move successfully through each developmental stage.

Some family support programs also reach out to families of school-age children, recognizing that these families, too, need support. As children get older, issues of school performance, parental authority, and negative peer pressure all become new sources of family stress. Programs often respond to these strains by offering such services as tutoring, study groups, and after-school activities directly to older children and teenagers. In addition, centers may offer short-term family counseling, hold group meetings for parents of school-age children, and plan special activities, field trips, and celebrations designed for the entire family.

What Are the Roots of Family Support?

Many historical and disciplinary threads are combined in the family support approach. The historical roots of family support programs reach back to the turn of the century and the settlement houses established by Jane Addams. Designed to serve the needs of new immigrants, the settlement houses recreated the sense of family and community the immigrants had left behind. The settlement house staffs also offered direct assistance in finding housing, employment, and medical care, while interpreting a sometimes mystifying culture to the disoriented immigrants.

> Social workers, educators, therapists, and health care professionals have come to see that they cannot protect, teach, or heal children in a vacuum.

A more recent influence on the development of family support programs was the social reform movement of the 1960s and 1970s, based in part on the conviction that recipients of services should participate in their design and delivery. In poor and minority communities across the country, civil rights workers, community activists, VISTA volunteers (Volunteers in Service to America), and others worked to create change through grassroots initiatives. Community-based literacy and self-help groups; cooperatives for food, shelter, and child care; and other local initiatives—some of which continue today—sought to substitute for the shortcomings of formal service systems.

For the family support movement, probably the most directly influential of all the 1960s-era programs has been Head Start, the comprehensive preschool program for disadvantaged children. Head Start's developers were the first to design a national education program acknowledging the interrelatedness of health, nutrition, parent involvement, and children's learning. They understood that getting the whole family involved at many different levels is the best way to sustain children's progress over time.

To help parents become better teachers for their children, Head Start asks each parent to volunteer some time as a Head Start classroom aide and to attend parent education meetings. Each Head Start program also is required to have a parent council with policy-making responsibilities. Today more than one-third of the Head Start's paid employees nationwide are former Head Start parents who were inspired to continue their education as a result of their participation in Head Start activities.

Every Head Start program includes a staff member whose job includes coordinating social services for participating families and providing assistance similar to that provided by family support workers. The social services coordinators are charged with helping families sort out all kinds of problems, helping parents develop education or employment plans, offering informal family counseling, and connecting families with other community resources and social services. In recent years, however, the national and regional Head Start offices have been concerned that too-large caseloads are making it difficult for Head Start social services coordinators to give all families adequate attention.

The Parent-Child Centers, funded under Head Start for low-income parents of infants and toddlers, also have been models for family support efforts. The centers were developed in response to research documenting the importance to healthy child development of a strong parent-infant bond and adequate physical and intellectual stimulation in the first years of life. Parent-Child Centers offer pregnant women and mothers of infants and toddlers either home visits, center-based activities, or both. Parents receive information and guidance to help them nurture their children and stimulate their development, health and nutrition education and assistance for the whole family, assistance with personal and economic problems, and help in obtaining other social services.

A series of federally supported demonstration programs initiated in the 1970s, which evaluated the effectiveness of the Parent-Child Centers, other variations of Head Start, and a number of comprehensive early childhood programs, provided a research basis for continuing the focus on early intervention efforts involving both children and parents.

More recently, renewed attention to effective means of supporting parents has emerged in the form of initiatives to assist teenage parents. Since many teen parents have had trouble in school and have yet to mature fully, programs that successfully help these parents provide such services as counseling, tutoring, parenting education, career planning, and help with day-to-day scheduling, transportation, and child care. These same broad-range services have proven effective in strengthening very needy and vulnerable families headed by older parents.

The roots of the family support movement have been multi-disciplinary. Social workers, educators, therapists, and health care professionals have come to understand that they cannot protect, teach, or heal children in a vacuum. These professionals increasingly focus on the family unit in efforts to prevent and treat child abuse and neglect, ensure children's success in school, and keep children healthy.

In health care, the long-established tradition of visiting nurses recognizes the importance of delivering individual treatment within a family context. Effective approaches to prenatal care, for example, include family-based outreach to pregnant women through home visitors, peer support groups, and mentoring relationships between experienced mothers and first-time mothers. Public health nurses and other home visitors also are playing useful roles in preventing child abuse and neglect by educating parents about age-appropriate expectations for children and helping parents enlarge their repertory of constructive responses to their children.

In education, parent involvement is an important component of the federally funded education programs for disadvantaged students and for students with disabilities. And home- and center-based literacy programs often focus on the needs of both parents and children.

Thus, the threads that form the fabric of many of today's family support programs have been spun out of many historical circumstances and experimentation within many disciplines. These threads have been woven together differently in diverse communities over the past two decades to meet the needs of particular children and families in particular circumstances.

Why Don't Existing Human Services Do the Job?

Family support has gained attention during the past decade as the shortcomings of our present human service system—including health, mental health, and other social service agencies—have created mounting frustration on the part of professionals, parents, child advocates, and others who care about children.

First, the present human service system is too often rigidly compartmentalized, with different bureaucracies and different funding streams designed to address specific problems of children and families. It's not unusual for social service or health agencies to have many separate locations and separate application and eligibility requirements. For example, in one county several years ago, a low-income family would have had to apply to 18 separate agencies to receive all of the services for which its members were likely to be eligible. Staff members in separate agencies often do not communicate with each other and are unaware of other services their clients are receiving. Such fragmentation makes it difficult to treat the whole family, to address more than one type of problem at a time, or to recognize and treat multiple problems comprehensively.

A social services manager recently described the case of a young boy who came to the attention of the child welfare system. He was having trouble in school, received some counseling through a mental health agency, and was taking Ritalin as prescribed by a physician. Neither the doctor, the counselor, nor the teacher had ever talked with one another about the boy's problems or progress.

Second, our social service system typically offers families nowhere to turn for help until family problems have gotten out of hand and a crisis develops. By that time, harm to family members is likely to have occurred and problems are difficult and costly to solve.

Yet family problems often start small and intensify over time. One problem builds upon another, especially when needs go unmet. The loss of a job or a reduced paycheck may lead to tension between parents, which may lead to alcohol abuse, which in turn eventually may lead to family violence or homelessness and cause a child to act out and get in trouble at school. At great expense, the city may place such a family in a homeless shelter or offer treatment for alcohol problems; the child may end up in trouble with the law and get placed in a costly detention center. Yet there is little help available to assist the parents early on with their employment, housing, or alcohol problems.

Similarly, many child protection agencies are overwhelmed by the numbers of children entering foster care as a result of parental abuse or neglect. However, little assistance is available for home visitor programs or respite care services, which are known to be effective in relieving family stress and preventing child abuse, or for intensive family preservation services that might protect the child, maintain the family unit while the family is working through a crisis, and avoid the need for costly out-of-home care.

Third, the current system is designed to help individuals, not families. A physician who prescribes a strict regimen of physical therapy for a disabled child might not understand why the mother doesn't follow it precisely. In fact, the mother might not understand the importance of the physical therapy, and she might be depressed by the family's crowded living conditions, which make it hard for her to find a quiet time and space for the exercises. The mother is not likely to follow the doctor's instructions until someone explains carefully why the therapy is necessary and until the family's housing situation improves. If someone doesn't take an interest in the *family,* the child's medical treatment may go nowhere.

The family support approach thus combines the wisdom gained from both our social service successes and failures. It seeks a humane, integrated, and effective means of helping families work through problems before they reach crisis proportions and interfere with children's healthy development and ability to learn. It seeks to build on the strengths of both families and communities.

Do Family Support Programs Deliver on Their Promises?

Evidence indicates that family support programs are improving the lives of participants. Many informal program assessments and innumerable stories describe individual families and children whose lives have been changed for the better. Most parents learn more about how their children develop and how to respond appropriately to their needs. Many parents get health care for themselves and their children and are connected with agencies that can provide special services to meet their children's special needs. Some parents are better able to cope with the daily demands of childrearing because they feel less isolated. And some parents develop the confidence they need to pursue educational and employment training opportunities that bring the whole family long-term benefits.

Evaluations of a range of family support initiatives, most using home visitors, generally have cited positive outcomes for children, especially on measures of health and development. When analyses of parenting practices were included in the studies, positive parenting behavior outcomes were found, as well. The recent evaluation of Missouri's Parents as Teachers program, probably the most extensive evaluation of recent family support initiatives, documents increases in parents' knowledge of child development and use of constructive childrearing practices, as well as positive effects on children's school-related development. In addition, an earlier generation of rigorous studies documented consistent positive outcomes from intensive early childhood education programs, many of which included home visiting or other forms of parental involvement and education.

Expanded research is under way to evaluate outcomes of family support programs across generations, to assess relationships among variables, and to examine long-term effectiveness. Meanwhile a number of states, confident the programs work, have moved to expand support efforts to reach more families and address their urgent, unmet needs. Such expansions suggest that those closest to the programs—families themselves, service providers, and program administrators—believe that supporting families before crises develop in many cases will prevent considerable child and family suffering and help avert the need for more costly services at a later time.

II

"There is no magic period of the life of a child. Each and every period is a magical and important one. . . . Our task, therefore, is not to find the right age to intervene, but the right intervention at each age."

Edward F. Zigler, *Handbook of Early Childhood Intervention*

Family Support Programs at Work

This section highlights a number of very different family support programs to suggest the many ways in which the family support approach can be implemented. These programs represent just a sampling of the hundreds that exist in communities across the country. They were selected to show the variety that exists in:

- The types of organizations and agencies that have developed and sponsored family support programs.
- The way the programs are funded.
- Program goals.
- The kinds of services that are offered and the methods used to deliver them.
- The communities that are served.
- The way family support programs supplement and augment existing social services in a community.

This section describes free-standing programs as well as family support efforts that have been added to programs originally developed for other purposes. A number of state initiatives to expand family support programs are mentioned, and state programs in Maryland and Missouri are described in some detail. Finally, there is a brief overview of the status of research on family support programs and a summary of what the research tells us to date about the benefits such programs offer children and parents.

Family Resource Centers

Family resource centers tend to be the most comprehensive among various family support efforts. Generally located in home-like buildings or converted houses, these centers serve as informal meeting places for regularly scheduled classes, groups, and social activities. As a rule, family resource centers offer such activities as support groups, parenting classes, child care, short-term counseling, recreational activities, prenatal education, and adult education classes. Some centers also have a home-visiting component and will refer families to other community resources for more specialized services. Community outreach and follow-up are essential components of these programs.

The five programs described here demonstrate how family resource centers develop to meet the needs of different communities: The Family Place, in Washington, D.C., serves families from Central America, including many new immigrants to this country. The Family Focus program in Lawndale, Illinois, operates in a low-income, largely black neighborhood of Chicago and serves many teenage parents. The Parenting Center in New Orleans is located in a hospital and primarily serves middle-class families in which many mothers do not work outside the home. The CEDEN Family Resource Center in Austin, Texas, serves predominantly Latino families. It has several components, one of which is a home-visitor program to prevent and reduce developmental delays in very young children. And the Survival Skills Institute in Minneapolis offers a variety of family support programs designed specifically to affirm the unique strengths of black families while meeting their differing needs.

The Family Place

The Family Place is family. Every weekday the red brick four-story house in a largely Spanish-speaking community in Washington, D.C., bustles with life and activity. Dozens of pregnant women and parents with young children—many of them recent immigrants—come to the Family Place to find the kind of caring help they probably would have gotten from their extended families back home.

Although the atmosphere is easy and informal, the Family Place is clear about its primary mission: to ensure women get early and regular prenatal care and parenting education, and that their young children get pediatric care. But those are not necessarily the reasons women first come to the Family Place, says Executive Director Maria Elena

Fostering an Appreciation of Differences

The New Community Family Place in a largely black neighborhood in Washington, D.C., brings needed family support services to that community. Like its parent program, New Community Family Place targets pregnant women and mothers of children younger than three. Parents and their young children may drop in at any time to use the play space and socialize with other families. New Community staff members offer on-site maternity preparation classes, prenatal exercise classes, infant development monitoring, and one-to-one counseling.

Family Place Executive Director Maria Elena Orrego says the new center will function as a demonstration effort to adapt the successful Family Place support program for Latinos to meet the needs of black families. "There are universal needs that every pregnant woman and every parent with young children has. However, the unique cultural and community strengths and values of the neighborhood will shape our programs and strategies," Orrego says. At Christmas, for example, the New Community not only organized a toy-making workshop but also offered families a chance to celebrate their African-American heritage at a Kwanzaa workshop.

"We have the opportunity to build bridges between these two culturally and ethnically diverse communities—communities that are often tragically pitted against each other," says Orrego. "We now have a chance to encourage and support parents in raising their children to appreciate and celebrate both communities' cultural, ethnic, and racial heritage."

The New Community Family Place
1312 8th Street, N.W.
Washington, DC 20001
(202) 265-1942

Orrego. Women usually come for specific help with a major crisis or for relief from physical and emotional stress. The Family Place serves any woman who is pregnant or has a child younger than three. There are no other eligibility requirements and services are free.

About 80 percent of the families that come to the center are Spanish-speaking, and about 17 percent are black. Because all of the classes and support groups are in Spanish, however, the Family Place offers non-Spanish-speaking families only emergency services, counseling, referrals to other agencies, and follow up. In response to the needs of black families, the Family Place in December 1991 opened a second family support center in a predominantly black neighborhood (see box, page 22).

A friend brought Anita to the Family Place because Anita's husband was drinking and abusing her. Anita had no means of support except her husband, she was six months' pregnant, and had a two-year-old daughter with cerebral palsy. A bilingual intake worker listened to Anita as she explained her family situation. The intake worker emphasized the importance of prenatal care and referred Anita to one of the four prenatal clinics in the area. Anita was informed about the legal rights and options for battered women in the city and was offered support if she decided to leave her home and go to a shelter.

The intake worker explained that the Family Place would provide transportation money if Anita needed it to reach a clinic or shelter, and a long-time participant or a staff member would accompany her if she wished. Before Anita left that day, she agreed to come back the next week to talk more about her daughter and other concerns.

Many of those who come to the Family Place are fearful and isolated from the larger community because of their undocumented status and inability to speak English, so their first visits are usually low-key. They can join other mothers chatting and playing on the floor with their toddlers in the bright first-floor playroom, and they are welcome to stay for a hot lunch, which is served every weekday. Gradually the new mothers develop friendships with other mothers and the staff members.

After Anita had her second interview, she was assigned a family services coordinator, and the two developed a plan to address the aspects of Anita's life that were causing her concern—her pregnancy, her daughter's problems, and her relationship with her husband. Although the Family Place focuses on pregnant women and mothers with children up to the age of three, the program also ensures that other family members are linked with services in the community.

During the next few months, Anita worked with her family services coordinator to enroll her daughter in a program for children with special needs. Anita and her worker explored several options to solve Anita's marital problems, including marital counseling and referring her husband to Alcoholics Anonymous.

Throughout her pregnancy, Anita was troubled. She was frightened that the baby might be damaged, and her marriage was not improving. However, the friendship and counsel she found at Family Place helped her keep her prenatal appointments at the clinic, and she attended the prenatal care classes at Family Place. Her baby was born healthy.

The classes in prenatal care, exercise, and parenting are the heart of the Family Place program. The prenatal care class is offered in six-week cycles, meeting once a week for an hour and a half to discuss topics such as nutrition or preparation for breastfeeding. When women reach the seventh month of pregnancy, they attend a four-week prenatal exercise class. This approach has ensured a good start in life for babies born to Family Place mothers. Very few babies are born at low birthweight (less than 5.5 pounds), a condition that is associated with a variety of health and development problems. In 1990, 158 babies were born to women assisted by the Family Place. The babies' average weight was more than 7.0 pounds, and only one was born prematurely.

The parenting class also meets once a week for six weeks. Topics of discussion include the emotional and physical development of infants and young children, and discipline. Staff members offer individual guidance sessions to parents who may be at risk of abusing or neglecting their children, and the Bebes Especiales project offers individualized services, including home visits, to families with children with identified disabilities.

Mothers also may attend weekly support group meetings to discuss issues chosen by participants, such as loneliness, adjusting to a foreign environment, and relationships with partners. Literacy classes and classes in English as a second language are offered to help prepare mothers for better paying employment.

Many of the activities and services offered at the Family Place are provided in conjunction with other service providers. For example, a Planned Parenthood staff member comes for half a day every week to help mothers with family planning issues. The Red Cross certifies parents as Red Cross babysitters, the Handicapped Infant Intervention Project provides a child development specialist for developmental screenings on a weekly basis, and a maternal and child health center sends its public health educator one afternoon a week to conduct a prenatal class.

A notable result of the program, says Orrego, is that once families become stable they often help others. Anita is a good example. After her baby was born, she decided to separate from her husband. Family Place helped Anita make arrangements to share an apartment temporarily with another participant. Several months later, when she and her children had found an apartment of their own, Anita, with backup from the Family Place, provided temporary shelter to another participant who needed a safe home during a transition. As a result of Family Place assistance and the generosity of Family Place participants such Anita, not one of the 45 homeless families that came to the Family Place in 1990 had to go to a city shelter.

The long-term goal of the Family Place is to break the cycle of poverty for children by enabling their parents to overcome the social and economic barriers they face in providing for their children's healthy development. So when it became clear that many Family Place mothers were having difficulty during childbirth at Washington's public hospital because there were no Spanish-speaking personnel in the delivery room, the Family Place staff assisted the mothers in taking their case to the public. According to former program director Joe Citro, the staff prepared a young mother to present the issue to a city-wide health forum. She captivated the audience with her own story, and the publicity that was generated prompted the hospital to hire Spanish-speaking staff members to translate forms and other vital information for patients.

The Family Place started in a church basement in 1981 as a project of the Church of the Saviour in Washington, D.C. It had two professional staff members, was funded primarily by the church and a foundation, and attracted mothers to the program by offering free use of a washing machine. In 1986 the Family Place Board of Directors raised and contributed enough money to purchase a permanent home for the program. In 1990 the staff of 16 served 457 families, with a budget of $434,000, about 56 percent of which comes from foundations, 11 percent from individuals, and 8 percent from churches. Government, businesses, and other organizations contribute the remainder.

The Family Place
3309 16th Street, N.W.
Washington, DC 20010
(202) 265-0149

Family Focus Lawndale

Another "classic" family resource center, Family Focus Lawndale pulls together many programmatic elements into a comprehensive collection of services for families and children. The center, which is one of a network of family resource centers in the Chicago area that make up Family Focus, Inc., offers drop-in services, discussion groups, educational workshops, life skills classes, social events, and other activities for interested families in this Chicago neighborhood.

Family Focus Lawndale's hallmark is the scale and intensity of its efforts, its exceptional community support and integration into the life of the neighborhood, and its close collaboration with several state-supported programs targeted at special populations. As do most family support centers, Family Focus Lawndale attributes its success to a highly committed, capable, and enthusiastic staff, some of whom are former program participants.

Started in 1983, Family Focus Lawndale originally was a small independent program focused on assisting pregnant and parenting teenagers in the largely black, low-income community, which had a teenage pregnancy rate much higher than the overall rate in Chicago. The center offered tutoring, personal growth and development groups, parent-child interaction groups, and the Minnesota Early Learning Design Curriculum for teenage mothers. In addition, Family Focus Lawndale staff trained young mothers who had been teenage parents to make home visits and conduct small discussion groups for pregnant and parenting teens.

Yvonne Heard, one of the early peer helpers, had a baby just a month or so before graduating from high school. A year later, in her role as a peer helper, she visited other pregnant teenagers once a week, ferrying their homework back and forth and sharing her own experience with pregnancy, labor, and infant care. One young girl told a newspaper reporter she didn't know how she would have weathered her pregnancy without Yvonne's visits. "She made me feel a whole lot better," said Patricia. "She'd bring me my homework, talk to me, and once the baby was born she showed me how to fix a bottle right. She was like a sister through this; there was hardly no one else I could count on."

The teenage mothers also participated in a Young Moms group at the center, which met one afternoon a week to share a meal of spaghetti or tacos and talk about common experiences and hopes for the future. The straight talk and the strong bonds that developed between the teens and their peer helpers motivated many of the new mothers to stay in school. Although about half of the girls at the local high school who gave birth did not return to school, most of those who participated in the Family Focus Lawndale program did.

News about the program spread quickly around the neighborhood, and soon younger siblings and cousins of the participating teenagers wanted a group of their own.

In response, the Family Focus Lawndale staff began offering programs for nonpregnant girls, aimed at preventing early pregnancy by building self-esteem and helping the girls set and carry out personal goals. Next, Family Focus Lawndale found funding to hire a male staff person to run a similar program for young men.

Today, Family Focus Lawndale is a large, comprehensive program. It acts as a catalyst to coordinate services for families in the community, working with more than 50 agencies, including social service agencies, hospitals, health centers, churches, and schools.

> "Once the baby was born she showed me how to fix a bottle right," said one young participant in the Family Focus Lawndale program, describing her peer helper. "She was like a sister through this; there was hardly no one else I could count on."

The center facilitates groups and activities for 350 junior and senior high school students. These primary prevention activities plus the continuing teen parents' program are funded through Parents Too Soon, a statewide pregnancy prevention and teen parent support program financed by the Illinois Ounce of Prevention Fund, a public-private agency.

Family Focus Lawndale is also the home of one of four state-funded pilot programs to improve school readiness for disadvantaged children. Project PIECE (Parents Implementing Education for Child Enrichment) is administered by the state Department of Education and uses home-based parent education programs to provide direct services to families with children from birth to age three. Each participating family receives weekly home visits for child development activities, and parents join discussion groups designed to help them give their children a strong foundation for learning.

In addition to providing these standard Project PIECE components, Family Focus Lawndale offers a supplementary Family Literacy program for its Project PIECE families. While their children attend Family Focus Lawndale's child care program or, if they are four, a preschool program at the neighboring elementary school, parents attend classes on computer literacy, home economics, parenting skills, and basic academic skills.

Family Focus Lawndale's staff members monitor the children's development and refer them for special services when needed. Staff members also help Project PIECE families identify and receive other social services for which they are eligible, housing assistance being one of the most requested. Family Focus Lawndale itself regularly provides emergency food for families using any of its services.

In 1990, 152 Lawndale families with 213 children participated in Project PIECE and Family Literacy. Most were AFDC families with more than one child. Families are referred by social service agencies or other participants.

Family Focus Lawndale conducts an annual evaluation of families that participate in its Project PIECE program. Results show that after six months in the program, parents' interactions with their children increase, parents give children more emotional and verbal cues on a regular basis, criticize and punish their children less, take their children on more outings, and are more likely to provide appropriate toys and play space.

An active Advisory Council representing community leaders, area residents, service providers, and business leaders supports the center by maintaining strong links between the program and the community. Director Gilda Ferguson says the council is "vital to

Family Focus Lawndale being a real community place." Through its committees on social services, education, health, and employment, the council brings problems facing center participants to the community and acts as a catalyst for community action.

Family Focus Lawndale operates on an annual budget of $850,000, most of which comes from the state to support the state-funded programs Lawndale runs on top of its basic drop-in services and classes for neighborhood residents. Family Focus Lawndale serves 650 families yearly in center-based programs, with a staff of 35.

Family Focus, Inc. began in 1976 with one center in Evanston, gradually adding programs over the years. All Family Focus centers are drop-in programs, with shared basic assumptions and approaches, but they differ in specifics as they respond to the culture of the families and neighborhoods they serve. Family Focus is committed to the concept that all families deserve a support system, so its programs are located in diverse neighborhoods, including a suburban community, a multi-ethnic and economically diverse community, and low-income areas with predominantly Latino and black populations.

As the parent organization, Family Focus is responsible for the administration, fund raising, and program development of its centers. Family Focus works with center directors to formulate plans and policies, provide on-going staff training, and assist in advocating on behalf of the families it serves.

Family Focus Lawndale
3600 West Odgen Avenue
Chicago, IL 60623
(312) 521-3306

Family Focus, Inc.
310 South Peoria Street
Suite 401
Chicago, IL 60607
(312) 421-5200

The Parenting Center at Children's Hospital

The Parenting Center at Children's Hospital offers preventive support services for families of young children in New Orleans. Founded in 1980 as a joint project of the Junior League and Children's Hospital, the center offers a drop-in program, community outreach, and a membership program of classes and workshops—many of which are open to the public for a small fee.

The drop-in center at the hospital is open six days a week. Parents bring their children for drop-in play groups, craft activities, and water play, supervised by parent and community volunteers. Parents either can participate with their children or have a cup of coffee and visit with other parents. Parent educators are present to observe the children and talk with mothers about child development issues. Between 12 and 30 families use center programs each day.

Most of the parents who drop in or attend classes are mothers of children younger than four who don't work outside the home and lack an extended network of relatives or friends with children. Some mothers are looking for adult companionship and encouragement. Others are having difficulties: a husband has lost his job or a child's toilet training is not going well. The more severe the troubles, the more time a parent educator spends with the parent, providing information, recommending classes, suggesting alternative ways of dealing with a problem or additional sources of assistance. The parent educators often call parents at home to see how things are going.

The center also has a Warm Line that anyone can call for advice and assistance. A trained parent volunteer calls back within 24 hours and either answers the caller's questions or provides a referral to another agency.

The center offers free, drop-in support groups for new parents and parents of twins. Workshops and classes are held quarterly on such basic topics as child development, discipline, nutrition, and positive communication. The center has an active Dads group and step-family programs. Field trips, special activities, and special classes on adoption, storytelling, breastfeeding, and CPR also are offered from time to time. The emphasis is on concrete, practical information and skill building. For a membership fee, parents can participate in a more extensive schedule of workshops and activities.

Through the Community Outreach Program, the center takes its services to parents who cannot participate during the day. The staff offers classes and workshops throughout the city, some of the most popular being the brown bag workshops held for working parents at their places of employment. At least half of those who attend are fathers. Staff members also give three- to six-week courses in parenting skills at churches and schools around the city.

Through all of its activities, the Parenting Center serves more than 4,000 families a year. There are seven full-time and part-time employees as well as 20 volunteers each semester. The center's budget of $140,000 is supported by foundations, fees, and fundraising activities. The center is a department of Children's Hospital, and the nonprofit hospital covers any budget deficit. An annual Halloween party for the community—Boo at the Zoo—raises $40,000 to $50,000 each year.

The Parenting Center
Children's Hospital
200 Henry Clay Avenue
New Orleans, LA 70118
(504) 896-9591

The CEDEN Family Resource Center

Ten years ago CEDEN's founder and executive director Emily Vargas Adams made a home visit to a single mother whose seven-month-old infant, Luis, was lying quietly in his crib. The mother, Maria, suffered from diabetes and seldom ventured outside the house. Luis was clean and well cared for, but he couldn't roll over or sit up. Testing revealed no physical problems.

"I could see this baby was loved," says Vargas Adams, "but the mother didn't hold him, and didn't talk to him. She was completely unaware of how to stimulate his development. He just lay there in his crib, all alone, day after day."

Without the CEDEN Parent-Child Program, Luis' mother might never have learned that an infant needs to be cuddled and bounced, talked to and praised in order to develop normally. By the time he started school, his developmental delays might have been difficult to overcome completely, even with special help.

But CEDEN intervened. Vargas Adams began to visit the family for at least an hour every week. While she played with Luis, demonstrating simple exercises to strengthen his muscles and develop his coordination, she talked with Maria about how infants grow and acquire new abilities. She brought toys, records, and books and showed the mother how to use them with Luis during the week. She encouraged the mother to take Luis out of the house and use the nearby park to enlarge his understanding of the world.

During the home visits they prepared finger foods so Luis could practice feeding himself. Vargas Adams talked about nutrition and home safety and answered the mother's questions about Luis' illnesses and behavior. Each time the home visitor came, she asked what new things Luis had done that week, what new sounds and words he was saying, and the three of them celebrated each new achievement.

Luis is now 10 years old. He is a happy, outgoing child who gets all As and Bs in school. His mother is committed to his education and helps out at his school despite her health problems. Occasionally the two of them stop by CEDEN to visit. "Maria changed from being a disengaged mother to being a highly engaged mother — always talking, reading, singing, and playing with her son," says Vargas Adams. "Engagement was the key."

CEDEN's mission is to promote and strengthen families through prenatal, early childhood, and parent education in the form of community-based, family-centered, and culturally comprehensive services. (CEDEN is the Spanish acronym for Center for the Development of Non-Formal Education, the program's original name.) The heart of CEDEN— and its original activity—is the home-based Parent-Child Program, which teaches parents how to prevent or reverse developmental delays in their infants and toddlers. At any one time, the Parent-Child Program serves about 30 children between infancy and 36 months of age and their families.

> "Maria changed from being a disengaged mother to being a highly engaged mother — always talking, reading, singing, and playing with her son."
>
> —Emily Vargas Adams

When a family is referred to the Parent-Child Program, staff professionals assess the child's development and the family's needs. The parents and an interdisciplinary team then develop an individualized family service plan that draws on CEDEN's resources and other community services. Most families participate in the program for about a year. By the time they leave the program, 85 percent of the children either have achieved or exceeded the developmental goals set for them. A three-year evaluation of infants who participated in 1984-1985 showed that CEDEN also was effective in encouraging parents to get formerly unimmunized children started on an immunization program. Since 1984 the Parent-Child Program has been replicated in four Texas locations, and the Texas Children's Trust Fund will be funding replications between 1992 and 1995.

Since the Parent-Child Program began serving families in 1979, CEDEN has added a variety of other services, including: an intergenerational learning center; a home- and school-based program for teenage parents; and help for families needing food and clothing, counseling for self-sufficiency, and referrals to other agencies.

Located between a black and a Latino neighborhood, CEDEN's two-story office building serves as a drop-in center and a meeting place for its parenting classes and social activities. About 70 percent of CEDEN's families are Latino, while the rest are non-Latino black or white. Most home visitors are bicultural and bilingual. When the center holds Black History Month celebrations, serving soul food and focusing on black parenting, Latina mothers attend just as enthusiastically as black mothers, says the director of the Parent-Child Program.

In its early years, CEDEN staff members went door-to-door to identify families with children who might have developmental delays. Today the program receives referrals from about 50 agencies, but Vargas Adams says she is reviving the practice of going door-to-door because CEDEN's early intervention specialists are able to identify delays earlier than personnel of most social service agencies.

CEDEN's Parent-Child Learning Center is open on Saturdays to all families in the neighborhood, and about 20 to 30 families come each week. The center offers basic education activities for both parents and children. Participants set their own goals. Much of the instruction is computer-assisted, which is especially popular with parents who have limited English-language skills. The learning center also offers classes in effective parenting and communication skills for all parents.

CEDEN operates a large toy lending library. Staff members explain how to use each toy to help children develop new abilities. CEDEN also has developed toy-making kits that enable parents to make their own toys from everyday items at home.

CEDEN's Prenatal Education Program, open to all families, matches each pregnant woman with a volunteer prenatal educator who visits the expectant mother four times in her home, once in the hospital, and at least once at home after the baby is born. The volunteer provides information about prenatal health care services, nutrition, fetal development, preparation for delivery, family planning, and baby care. CEDEN offers similar parenting and child development services to teenagers through the Del Valle Independent School District in Austin.

All told, CEDEN serves more than 900 families each year. In 1991 CEDEN had 22 staff members and a total budget of $650,000, a significant expansion from the $12,000 program it operated during its first year in 1979. The Parent-Child Program, which costs between $900 and $1,200 per target child per year, is funded by the state's Early Childhood Intervention Program, the City of Austin, Travis County, and the United Way. Other funders include national and local foundations, the Texas Education Agency, and many corporations, churches, and families.

CEDEN Family Resource Center
1208 East 7th Street
Austin, TX 78702
(512) 477-1130

Survival Skills Institute and the Black Family Parenting Education Program

Helping black families reach within themselves to find and act on their strengths—that's the mission Dr. Geraldine Carter envisioned for the Survival Skills Institute in Minneapolis when she opened its doors in a then-rundown house in a tough Minneapolis neighborhood in 1979. Carter's work in the public schools and in mental health services had convinced her that existing social services didn't speak to the culture and environment in which black families live.

Survival Skills' first program, FREEDOM, was designed to help heal and reunite families and children who had been separated as a result of child abuse or neglect. Out of FREEDOM came PACT, a preventive parent education and support effort to help parents improve their parenting skills before it became necessary to place their children in foster care. A third program, NEST, combines a specialized half-day active learning experience for children having difficulty in kindergarten with a home-visiting program to involve their parents in their education.

As new programs were developed to meet the different needs of families, Survival Skills began acquiring neighboring homes to house them. Dorothy Johnson, executive director, says Survival Skills uses renovated houses because they are less forbidding than offices and because the tidy houses themselves serve as positive models for program participants and for the larger community. Survival Skills now owns four houses in a row, (one of which had been a crack house) and has, in essence, conducted its own blockwide urban renewal project. "When we first moved into the neighborhood, the street looked bombed out," says Johnson. "Now the entire block is nice-looking."

Carter says "environmental therapy" is an important part of Survival Skills' programs. "When parents and children come into our buildings, they see people who look like them, and everything stresses, 'You are welcome. This is where you belong.'"

In 1988 Survival Skills received three-year funding from the McKnight Foundation to reach out to families in a new way. Carter enlisted the help of eight black churches to offer a new Black Family Parenting Education Program (BFPEP) to strengthen families in low-income neighborhoods in Minneapolis and St. Paul. Each church received an annual $500 stipend for housing, publicizing, and supporting the program. Participants were drawn from the churches' own congregations and from the surrounding community.

The decision to offer the program through black churches was based on Carter's belief that a culturally comfortable context would increase parents' interest in participating. In conversations with program evaluators, a number of participating parents later agreed, with several saying they hadn't been interested in attending until they realized the class would meet at church.

During each 19-week course, groups of eight to 12 parents—fathers as well as mothers—gathered at neighborhood churches on Monday evenings from six until nine to talk about raising children. Many of the churches provided child care so parents could bring their children along. Parents discussed child development and parenting skills for each stage of a child's life from birth to age six. At home, parents read five short, easy-to-read parenting manuals, specially written by Carter for black parents, which included child development activities parents could do with their children on their own.

Survival Skills trained two new volunteers from every participating church to lead each 19-week session. Except for the first session's volunteers, the trainers were parents who had taken the class previously. Each participating church now has a cadre of volunteers with considerable substantive knowledge and administrative skill as a result of their involvement in BFPEP.

The group discussions were always lively, says a volunteer trainer. "These parents haven't had opportunities to talk to each other—not just about parenting but about life. We laughed, we cried some, and we prayed some," the volunteer says. As the discussions caused parents to remember their own childhoods, some painful feelings and memories surfaced. The group members comforted and supported each other, says the volunteer, and began to believe that their children's lives could be different. A December 1991 impact evaluation of the program noted that the "most salient issues of parenting revolved around the experience of being black."

On the whole, say several volunteer trainers, parents were open to new ideas about childrearing. One young father came into the class boasting about how independent his two-year-old was, one trainer recalls. The child turned on the hot water for his bath, got his own food—even cut his own piece of cake with a knife. After the group discussed why it's dangerous for a two-year-old to be doing these things, the father changed his parenting practices and tried to spend more time with his son.

"It's a matter of awareness," says another volunteer trainer. "The course got us to think about what we're used to doing without thinking." For example, she says, most parents haven't thought about using feeding time to give children attention and affection. Especially if parents are tired, she says, the temptation is to put the food in front of the child and turn on the television. But in the course, the leader introduced the importance of making feeding a time of teaching and love, whatever the child's age.

As each course progressed, parents typically began to form their own support network—calling each other, helping out with transportation and child care, celebrating birthdays, and bringing in ideas and materials to share in class. Once parents began to see the possibility of change, says one volunteer, they wanted training in other areas. One class, for example, decided to bring in a nurse to teach CPR.

Reaching Out to Fathers
Fatherhood Project, Avancé Family Support and Education Program

Over and over again, directors of family support programs emphasize the need to find ways of effectively including fathers and mothers' partners. It's difficult for a mother to modify established family patterns and take greater charge of her own life if her partner isn't comfortable with the changes that are taking place in the family. Yet for many reasons, most fathers do not get involved readily in family support activities unless the program makes special efforts to include them—and even those efforts are not always successful, according to many family support staff members.

Gloria Rodriguez, director and founder of the Avancé program in San Antonio, Texas, which serves primarily Latino families, decided in 1987 to address the issue of fathers' participation head on by developing a program specifically for fathers.

Isaac Cardenas, who was hired to design and run the new project, found that fathers were not as readily responsive to opportunities for self-improvement as were the mothers who came to the center. Men were more attracted to one-time activities they could share with their children—sports and scouting activities, for example, or field trips. Yet after participating in these kinds of activities for a time, many fathers seemed to become more interested in attending classes and small group meetings, especially if they were just for fathers and were led by men. So Cardenas designed the Fatherhood Project to expand gradually fathers' involvement in the center's activities.

Now the project offers all-male parenting groups, where the fathers discuss such topics as children's emotional needs, discipline practices, and children's homework. As the men become more comfortable with each other, they begin to confront deeper issues such as family violence, alcoholism, and depression. The discussions are aimed at helping fathers improve their ability to communicate with family members, control their anger, and find productive ways of coping with stress. Over time a special ritual has developed: At the beginning of the series of group meetings the men make a pledge of nonviolence in front of the group, and at the end of the series they make the same pledge in front of their wives and partners.

The three-year foundation-funded pilot program in Minneapolis/St. Paul, which served a total of about 160 parents, ended in September 1991. Now BFPEP is going nationwide. Relevant Education Corporation in Arlington, Virginia, is distributing the materials and conducting train-the-trainer workshops for churches and other interested community organizations.

Some of the original participating churches hope to continue the program despite the loss of the stipend. One enthusiastic pastor says, "Whatever it takes, we'll have this program 'til Jesus comes."

Survival Skills Institute
1501 Xerxes Avenue North
Minneapolis, MN 55411
(612) 522-6654

Relevant Education Corporation
4665 South 4th Street
Arlington, VA 22204
(703) 920 7006

Another goal of the project is to offer fathers a chance to improve their literacy. Again in all-male classes, fathers spend one hour a week on parenting skills and a second hour on English language skills or on preparation for a GED. Cardenas says many fathers succeed in this class who have not done well in other literacy programs.

Cardenas tries to make it easy for fathers to participate. For example, classes and activities are planned around fathers' work schedules. Cardenas contacts fathers at home to work out scheduling problems and encourage participation. The project also provides transportation to meetings for those who need it.

About 50 fathers at a time participate weekly in the intensive phase of the program, which lasts nine months. At the end of that time, they receive a certificate of accomplishment, but they are welcome to continue participating in any classes or activities that interest them.

Cardenas says he sees changes in the men who become involved in the project—and in their families, as well. The family usually becomes more unified, the parents are more likely to share in decision making, and family conflicts are handled in more positive ways. The fathers interact with their wives or partners and with their children more gently and with greater respect, says Cardenas. And when the men find themselves facing a tough problem, they are likely to come in to talk about it.

The message the Fatherhood Project tries to get across, says Cardenas, is, "We don't have much, but let's make the most of what we have for our children." And, he adds, by helping fathers help their children, the project hopes to inspire the fathers to take new steps toward realizing their own dreams.

Avancé Family Support and Education Program
435 South San Dario
San Antonio, TX 78237
(512) 431-6600

Home-Visitor Programs

Many programs use home visitors either exclusively or primarily to extend preventive help and support to families. Home-visitor programs are driven by various goals: some emphasize prenatal education and support for mothers to ensure healthy births; others are designed to prevent child abuse and neglect; some focus on promoting healthy child development and preparation for school success. Still others strive to achieve all of these goals.

Sometimes the home visitors are trained paraprofessionals, sometimes they are nurses or other professionals. The frequency and duration of the visits vary by program and often are determined by the family's needs. Some but not all programs use regular group meetings to supplement the home visits, and some programs offer center-based drop-in activities, as well.

Although each of the four programs described here has a slightly different focus, part of the home visitors' job in each program is to link families with additional services in the community so that multiple family needs are addressed and overall family functioning is strengthened.

MIHOW (Maternal Infant Health Outreach Worker) Project

Life is hard for families in the Mississippi Delta and Appalachia. Unemployment and poverty are enduring facts of life. The search for employment is likely to separate or uproot families, and health care and social services often are far away.

The MIHOW Project was created in 1982 to serve rural families in this part of the country. Its goals are to improve prenatal and infant care among families that don't fully utilize health clinics, and to help solve the complex problems of the region by enhancing the development of its human resources.

MIHOW is a network of family support programs organized by the Center for Health Services (CHS) at Vanderbilt University in cooperation with the Clinch River Education Center in Abingdon, Virginia. The local sponsoring agencies are rural health clinics, community development agencies, and other community organizations in Tennessee, Kentucky, Virginia, and West Virginia.

The success of each MIHOW program rests in large part on its outreach workers—the natural helpers in the community. These women know about early pregnancy, long-term unemployment, isolation, and feelings of inadequacy and hopelessness, for those realities have been as much a part of their own lives as they are a part of the lives of the families they visit. Yet the outreach workers also hold up an example of strength, determination, and community service.

Even with roots in their communities, the outreach workers have to build trust slowly among the families they serve. "The people in our area don't trust just anybody," one outreach worker told a program evaluator during a 1990 qualitative evaluation of MIHOW. "They have been exploited so much it's hard for them to give their trust at first."

But gradually the outreach workers gain the mothers' confidence. "It was like making a new friend," one mother said during the evaluation. "Someone you could share your feelings and thoughts with, without having to do a lot of explaining." In focus groups and interviews, mothers reported that they felt less isolated and more in charge of their lives after starting the program, and their relationships with their spouses and children had improved.

Most of the parents who participate in the programs are young; the average age is about 20 at the birth of the MIHOW-targeted child. Two-thirds of the participating mothers are white and one-third are black. Almost half are married and live with their husbands. Most have not completed high school.

The outreach worker typically begins to visit a family while the mother is pregnant and continues until the child is two years old. At some sites home visiting continues until the child is three and eligible for Head Start. At most sites the outreach worker comes monthly, starting before a baby is born and continuing until the baby's first birthday. After that, the visits are every other month. Parents also are invited to attend regular parents' meetings and special activities.

The outreach worker has a curriculum to guide her, but she also responds to each family's unique needs. She may take along a VCR to show a pregnant mother a video on breastfeeding, something that is uncommon in this part of the country. She may take books to read to the children. A mother whose youngest is now three and who therefore doesn't receive frequent visits any longer said, "We miss [the workers' visits]. My kids miss them—the participation—and they always taught them something.... They called them parties and they always educated the kids, too."

> The parenting class was helpful, said one mother, because it gave her "insight to understand that children are people too. You give them choices instead of demanding this and demanding that..."

Unmarried teenagers who become pregnant frequently are ostracized by disapproving parents, and some mothers are so angry with their daughters they object to visits by the outreach worker. Yet some outreach workers have been able to help families resolve tensions and have given the daughters emotional support while their families adjusted to the new situation. One teenager said, "When [the MIHOW worker] would come by the house my mama would create an awful scene.... My mama would tell her she was wasting her time on me because I was no good and hopeless. One day [the MIHOW worker] talked to my mama by herself, and I heard my mama crying and saying she was scared for me.... After that she was always nice to [the MIHOW worker] and me too."

In addition to providing help with health and childrearing problems, the outreach workers encourage family members to take advantage of other resources in the community, including GED and literacy classes and social services for which they are eligible. One woman told evaluators, "MIHOW made me better able to cope with the system. They have strengthened me a lot." Another pregnant mother told of her difficulty with the Medicaid bureaucracy and how the outreach worker had given her the confidence to "keep getting on them" until she finally got results.

Assessments of MIHOW show that participation leads parents to change their behavior in ways that benefit their children's development. One evaluation based on the Caldwell HOME inventory documented that MIHOW mothers are more emotionally and verbally responsive to their children, provide more appropriate play materials, are more involved in helping their children achieve knowledge and skills that are age-appropriate, are more accepting of their children's behavior, and provide more opportunities for their children to interact with a variety of adults. The Caldwell HOME inventory, an assessment of parent-child interaction and home environment based on observation and parent interviews, has been demonstrated to correlate positively with children's later school performance.

In addition, during the 1990 qualitative study of MIHOW, many mothers themselves emphasized how much they had learned about childrearing, both from the home visitors and from parents' groups and meetings. "[The MIHOW program] has helped with my self-confidence," said one mother. "When we talked about how to deal with [her child's] temper tantrums it helped me. I could be a lot calmer about it. I could handle it better." The parenting class was helpful, said another mother, because it gave her "insight to understand that children are people too. You give them choices instead of demanding this and demanding that.... This is kind of hard to put in effect. But it has been planted in there and it does make a difference."

The developers of the MIHOW project hoped that the local programs would become financially self-sufficient and would serve as catalysts for new community activities and services for families. With this goal in mind the outreach workers receive training in fund raising and program planning—and with good results. All of the original five local programs were able to raise enough money from local, state, and private sources to continue operating after the initial start-up funding ran out. Four of these five continued to operate a MIHOW project as of late 1991. Three additional programs are receiving start-up funding.

The Center for Health Services (CHS) and the Clinch River Education Center jointly are responsible for training the outreach workers. They provide both initial and ongoing training in the areas of prenatal health, child development and parenting, nutrition, and home safety. Each MIHOW site has one to four outreach workers and serves between 20 and 80 families.

CHS also continues to work with all of the local projects on program and organizational planning and management, curriculum development, fund raising, and evaluation. Several of the programs have broadened their outreach to cover other health issues such as heart disease and black lung disease. And other MIHOW programs have added toddlers' groups, day care programs, and literacy projects.

MIHOW
Center for Health Services
Station 17, P.O. Box 567-VUH
Nashville, TN 37232-8180
(615) 322-4773

Ewa Healthy Start Program

Almost three years ago, when Mary was in the hospital for the birth of her ninth child, a staff member from the Ewa Healthy Start Program on Hawaii's island of Oahu suggested she might benefit from participating in the program's home visitor program. There were indications the baby might have been exposed prenatally to drugs, one of Mary's high-school-aged daughters had been sexually abused by her father and by Mary's boyfriend, and the family was in therapy with another agency.

Although Mary agreed to participate, she was resistant and uncooperative for the first year, and the Ewa worker, fearing for the children's well-being, asked child protective services to get involved with the family.

About that time, a new Ewa worker was assigned to Mary's family. She was a grandmother and the two women bonded very quickly. After several months, Mary told the Ewa program staff that the support worker was the best friend she ever had. With the support worker's encouragement, Mary found a four-bedroom apartment for her family and moved out of her boyfriend's apartment. Mary's baby began improving, and the four-year-old was enrolled in the home-based Head Start program.

Today, says Ewa Program Director Elaine Chu, the family is doing much better. The older children are having few problems in school, and although the baby, now almost three, has some developmental delays, a public health nurse keeps a close eye on his development.

"Mary and her children still have a long way to go," says Chu, "but their progress has been amazing. Mary's attitude about herself has improved—we can see the change in her face. And she is making positive changes in her life."

The Ewa Healthy Start Program at Ewa Beach began in 1985 as a state demonstration program in Hawaii's search for a strategy to prevent juvenile delinquency and other problems resulting from an abusive, disadvantaged childhood. The Ewa program was designed by the Hawaii Family Stress Center at the Kapiolani Medical Center for Women and Children in Honolulu, which already had been using home-visitor services to improve family functioning and reduce the incidence of child abuse for more than a decade.

The Ewa demonstration program was found to be so successful that the state used it as a model for the state-funded Healthy Start/Family Support Services program established in 1988. In 1991 the Family Stress Center and six other private agencies operated a total of 12 community-based home-visitor programs on Oahu and five neighbor islands. The addition of five new sites was planned for 1992.

Participation in Ewa, as in all Healthy Start/Family Support Services programs, is voluntary. Families of newborns are screened for family risk factors such as unstable housing, histories of substance abuse, depression, parents' abuse as a child, late or no prenatal care, less than 12 years of schooling, poverty, and unemployment. Early Identification (EID) Workers, who are trained paraprofessionals, screen and interview new mothers in the hospital. They also screen and interview families referred by physicians, public health nurses, and others. Because the demand for services outstrips the available resources, only families with a substantial number of risk factors may participate.

Each newly participating family receives a weekly visit from an Ewa family support worker. Each of Ewa's eight home visitors works with approximately 25 families at a time. All of the family support workers and EID workers are specially trained members of the community who are able to approach families as concerned neighbors and fellow parents.

Since many families initially are in considerable distress as a result of such problems as unemployment, lack of adequate housing, or substance abuse, the support worker's first task often is to help the family cope with immediate crises. For example, the support worker may help the family obtain housing assistance or enroll in Medicaid or in the WIC nutrition program. The worker also links the family directly with a pediatrician to ensure that children receive regular health care, are screened for developmental delays, and are immunized on schedule. Pediatricians have been oriented to the program and are notified when a child is enrolled in Healthy Start and when a family still considered to be at risk stops participating.

In the beginning, the support workers take much of the initiative, but as the family situation stabilizes they encourage parents to become more and more active in monitoring family needs, securing necessary services, and taking responsibility for achieving the goals they set for their families.

What Businesses and Civic Groups Can Do To Assist Family Support Programs

What businesses can do:
- Donate services such as taxicab rides to parent meetings, and donate furniture, play equipment, infant care equipment, and office equipment for family support centers.
- Donate space for parent meetings, child care, and family support programs.
- Donate administrative aid and support for program administration. Provide secretarial, bookkeeping, and publishing assistance.
- Donate public relations and fund-raising expertise.
- Arrange workshops with family support staff members for employees with families.
- Recruit volunteers to help with special projects and events.
- Adopt a family support center and build a long-term partnership. Hire participating parents when possible.
- Provide funding to help a community-based agency start a new family support center in an unserved neighborhood.
- Advocate for family support programs at the local and state levels.

What religious organizations and civic groups can do:
- Donate space for parent meetings, child care, and family support programs.
- Organize volunteers to make toys and baby blankets or assemble packages of necessities for newborns and donate them to a family support program.
- Collect used baby equipment and children's clothing for donation to family support programs.
- Organize fund-raising events for family support programs.
- Assist a family support program with its community outreach.
- Adopt a family support program and establish a long-term partnership.
- Organize volunteers to help with building renovation and maintenance.
- Recruit volunteers to help with special projects and events.
- Encourage members to serve as mentors for families being served by the family support program.
- Sponsor a parent education course at a local school or church in partnership with a family support program.
- Advocate for family support programs at the local and state levels.

As trust is established between the family and the family support worker, the visits begin to focus on the parent-child relationship, child development, and parenting skills, but progress is not always easy. One couple, for example, steadfastly refused to acknowledge that drugs, health problems, unemployment, and family violence were destroying their family and harming their children. Fearing for the children's safety, the Ewa worker called in child protective services, which removed the children from the family.

Very soon, however, the mother called the worker to thank her. She said it wasn't until their children were taken away that she and her husband began to realize what they were doing. As the support worker continued to work with the family, the mother stopped using drugs and the father found a job, went into therapy, and is learning how to manage his anger. The family has been reunited and the children are doing well.

The Ewa program recently hired a child development specialist to work with families of children with special needs. And in some cases, the program's male family support worker also visits a father specifically to talk about his role in the family.

The support workers encourage parents to participate in group activities held each week at the Ewa Center located in a neighborhood shopping center. From time to time, the center also organizes special activities and field trips for families. Frequently these activities provide the family's only social contacts.

Families may participate in Healthy Start/Family Support Services programs until the child is five and enters public school, and about 40 percent of Ewa families participate that long. Family needs and changes are evaluated at regular intervals. As families become stronger, home visits become less frequent—perhaps only once a month or once a quarter.

The Ewa pilot program documented success in preventing child abuse. Among the 241 high-risk families served during the three years of the demonstration program, there were no cases of child abuse and only four cases of neglect. The Ewa staff referred five families to child protective services for intensive assistance, and actual abuse was prevented in every case. In contrast, among families identified as high risk but not served because of inadequate resources, the rate of abuse was three times higher than in the general population.

The Ewa program's annual budget is approximately $400,000, and the program cost per family is estimated to be $2,100 per year. The Maternal and Child Health Branch of the state Department of Health provides 98 percent of the funding, with additional support coming from private foundations and local fund-raising events.

The 12 Healthy Start/Family Support Services programs are linked through quarterly meetings and a variety of networking activities. The Hawaii Family Stress Center provides staff training for all of the sites. Home visitors attend an initial five-week training course as well as a five-day session after six months on the job. At monthly in-service meetings, home visitors discuss issues that arise during their family visits and receive more specialized training.

Ewa Healthy Start Program
91-902 Fort Weaver Road, #P105
Ewa Beach, HI 96706
(808) 689-8371

Hawaii Family Stress Center
1833 Kalaaua Avenue
Suite 1001
Honolulu, HI 96815
(808) 947-5700 or 944-9000

The Family Outreach Program

The Johnsons had a newborn and four other children ages two through five when the visiting nurse came to see the Warwick, Rhode Island, family for the first time. Mr. Johnson, at age 28, was unemployed and recovering from a heart attack. He was depressed and verbally and physically abusive to his family. Living conditions were crowded, and there wasn't enough money for food. The five-year-old was not enrolled in school. Mrs. Johnson was emotionally and physically exhausted.

At the time of the baby's birth, a routine hospital screening of newborns and their families by a public health nurse had identified the Johnsons as a high-risk family and likely to benefit from help aimed at strengthening their parenting skills and promoting the baby's healthy development. The family was referred to the state Health Department's Family Outreach Program in Kent County. The program contracts with a visiting nurse agency to visit high-risk families with newborns. If a family is interested in participating, the nurse visits regularly for up to a year to monitor the infant's physical and developmental progress, offer the parents support and information to help them nurture their children, and link the family with other appropriate community services.

In the Johnsons' case, the nurse began visiting weekly because the family was experiencing extreme stress. A nurse might visit a less vulnerable family only once or twice a month, or a family with a medically fragile infant several times a week.

With the Johnsons, the nurse first helped enroll the family in the state's public assistance program. Then she connected the family with a social worker and a mental health worker to make sure the family received the special services they needed. Next she assisted the parents in registering the five-year-old for school and enrolling the four-year-old in Head Start. The three-year-old was enrolled in Early Start, a federally funded child development program that provides both a home visit by an early childhood education specialist and a group meeting for parents every week. And after conducting a preliminary developmental assessment of the two-year-old, the nurse referred him to the state's early intervention program, which has a strong parent-to-parent support component.

At the time this publication was being prepared, the nurse had been visiting the Johnsons every week for almost six months to monitor the baby's health and development, support and encourage the parents, and check in on the older children. The family was continuing to have enormous problems, according to the nurse, although it had been possible to provide enough support to avoid the placement of the children in foster care.

After a family participates in Family Outreach for six months, a nurse conducts a comprehensive assessment of the family, the home environment, and the infant's development. The nurse's findings are reviewed by a multidisciplinary team composed of the visiting nurse and professionals from such agencies as Head Start, the school system, child welfare, mental health, and the state early intervention program. At this stage, many infants are referred to the early intervention program, which accepts children at risk of or exhibiting signs of developmental delays. If it seems appropriate and other family supports are firmly in place, the team may recommend that the family's participation in Family Outreach be phased out and that another agency take over case management. However, if the family is still having medical, parenting, or other problems that call for close monitoring and support, the nurse continues to visit the family and play the role of case manager.

The Johnsons' visiting nurse says the families generally wean themselves from the program after a year or so. By then, she says, "most parents have become empowered to advocate for their own children." They have developed an understanding of normal growth and development and parenting techniques and are able to recognize if and when their family needs further assistance. The nurses also have informed the parents about the help that's available and shown them how to get it.

In the Kent County area near Providence, there are about 3,000 live births each year. Approximately 85 percent of the families are screened in the hospital at the time of the birth by a public health nurse. About 29 percent are found to be at risk as a result of such factors as limited or no prenatal care, prematurity or low birthweight, or the young age, low education level, or employment, medical, or drug problems of the parents. Every at-risk family is referred to the Family Outreach Program and visited by a maternal and child health nurse to see if the family wants to participate. Physicians and others may refer families to the program, and there also are some self-referrals. More than 75 percent of referred families choose to participate, and some of those who initially decline later join. The five nurses in the Kent County program each serve between 40 and 60 families at a time, although not all of the families are served intensively.

> A nurse might visit a less vulnerable family only once or twice a month, or a family with a medically fragile infant several times a week.
>
> ◆

About 30 percent of the families in the Family Outreach Program have premature infants that require skilled nursing assessment and monitoring, says maternal and child health nurse Maureen Claflin. These tiny babies have severe respiratory problems, and many are still hooked up to an oxygen supply when they go home. Neurological immaturity makes them hypersensitive and vulnerable to overstimulation, and it's difficult for parents to know how to meet their special needs without supportive teaching and modeling. The visiting nurses from the Family Outreach Program not only provide the specialized medical information that parents of "premies" need, they offer encouragement and assistance with other problems at the same time.

Larry was born more than three months premature as a result of complications from his mother's diabetes. When he left the hospital at 12 weeks, he was dependent on oxygen, needed physical therapy, and had to be fed every hour around the clock, says Claflin, who was the family's visiting nurse. She visited the family every day for two months, supporting the exhausted and distraught first-time parents, explaining Larry's needs, and teaching the parents how to calm him and read his cues so they could avoid overstimulating him.

Claflin recognized that the parents needed additional support and encouragement, so she also linked them with a social worker and with a parent support group sponsored by the state early intervention program. Larry had his first birthday at the end of 1991, and although he is small, he is developing into a healthy, thriving child.

The Family Outreach Program in the Providence area is one of two state pilot programs designed to bring the state health department's long-time nurse home-visiting program in line with current thinking about coordinated community-based human services. The three-year-old pilots introduced a new emphasis on linking families to a broad range of community resources and established mechanisms, including the family review teams, for interagency coordination and collaboration in service delivery.

The approach pioneered by the pilots is now being introduced into the nurse visiting program statewide. Beginning early in 1992, the state hopes to begin screening the families of all 15,000 or so infants born in the state each year for referral to the Family Outreach Program. The cost of the program's services are covered largely by Medicaid, the federal Maternal and Child Health Block Grant, and state appropriations.

Family Outreach Program
Kent County Visiting Nurse Association
51 Health Lane
Warwick, RI 02886
(401) 737-6050

HIPPY (Home Instruction Program for Preschool Youngsters)

Every two weeks in Monticello, Arkansas, in the rural southeast corner of the state, 30 specially trained women each visit 15 mothers of preschoolers and kindergarten-age children living within their respective school districts. Many of these families are very poor and isolated from other families. The home visitors are paraprofessionals from the HIPPY program, designed to boost the overall well-being, school readiness, and eventual school success of four- and five-year-olds. Most of these home visitors are themselves mothers of young children and all are members of the community. They are trained to listen and give support to the families they visit, and to offer information and materials parents can use to encourage their children's healthy development.

During each home visit, the paraprofessionals use the HIPPY curriculum to strengthen the mothers' understanding of child development, parenting techniques, nutrition, and health and safety issues. The home visitors leave an activity packet and a storybook for the mothers to use with their child for 15 minutes each day during the next week. The packets contain materials designed to help mothers stimulate their child's ability to think logically and solve problems. They also include activities that teach such things as new vocabulary words, how to recognize shapes and colors, and how to sort objects by size. The home visitors role play the activities for the mothers.

During the alternating weeks, when the paraprofessionals don't make home visits, participating mothers attend a small group meeting held at their local school. There they review the previous week's lesson and discuss related issues with the HIPPY coordinators and other mothers. HIPPY program coordinators often invite pediatricians, school counselors, child development specialists, kindergarten teachers, and others to come and talk with the mothers. Transportation and child care are provided for mothers who need them to attend.

HIPPY group meetings in rural Arkansas are intended not only to reinforce the material presented during the home visits, but also to offer mothers opportunities to develop new social and interpersonal skills and reduce feelings of isolation. Sometimes, says HIPPY Coordinator Judy Gibson, the discussions at the group meetings become very personal and lead to significant changes.

At one meeting, for example, a school counselor had come to talk with the mothers about the social and emotional needs of children entering kindergarten. That discussion led the mothers to begin talking about their own feelings of inadequacy. One mother, Joan, said she had never hugged any of her five children or told them she loved them.

During the following weeks, Joan, her home visitor, and a HIPPY coordinator talked about Joan's behavior toward her children and her desire to show more affection. Eventually, Joan decided to try to hug each of her children every day. At first, the children were confused and resisted their mother's affection, especially her 10-year-old son, who had been identified as very depressed and was receiving help from other state agencies. But Joan stuck to her promise and slowly the children began to respond. After a while, the four-year-old, who participated in the HIPPY program, began to repeat the same messages of affirmation and appreciation that Joan was learning to use. It became clear that the family atmosphere was changing fundamentally when the little girl began to tell Joan, "I love you, Mommy. You are so special to me."

Now Joan and her family are doing well. Her youngest child is five and enrolled in kindergarten, but Joan stays involved in HIPPY by going over the HIPPY lessons with a four-year-old girl she babysits. Joan also has recruited two other families into the HIPPY program.

In the Monticello area, the three-year-old HIPPY program is sponsored by the Southeast Arkansas Education Service Cooperative, composed of 14 school districts. By joining forces, the school districts are able to share the costs of the program yet keep it rooted in individual communities, offering services through each school district. The staff of three professional coordinators and 30 paraprofessionals serve more than 500 families each year.

The educational cooperative recruits participating families by sending announcements home from school with students; posting announcements in local churches, public buildings, and Laundromats; and sending the paraprofessional staff door-to-door to identify families with four- and five-year-olds. Interested families are asked to commit themselves to two years' participation, including the year before a child goes to kindergarten and the kindergarten year itself. Some families leave the program after one year, often because they leave the area in search of better economic opportunities. However, some mothers stop participating because they believe the school will take over responsibility for their child's progress, so the program is stressing the importance of parents' continued involvement in their children's learning.

The paraprofessionals must be former HIPPY mothers or must know a four- or five-year-old child with whom they can work. Although they don't need a high school diploma or a GED, the paraprofessionals do need to have appropriate reading skills, the ability to listen to and support the families they serve, and the ability to organize activities. The paraprofessionals receive three days of initial training and attend weekly in-service meetings to review the coming week's lesson and watch the coordinators role play the activities. They also attend occasional statewide HIPPY training meetings.

The HIPPY program in the United States—HIPPY USA—is sponsored by the National Council of Jewish Women, headquartered in New York, and is adapted from a program originally developed in Israel for new immigrant families. The state of Arkansas actively promotes the program and is working with HIPPY USA to adapt the curriculum materials for the American context. At present there are 30 HIPPY programs in Arkansas sponsored by various organizations, including six educational cooperatives. The network is coordinated through the Arkansas Children's Hospital HIPPY Center in Little Rock, a regional training and technical assistance center. The state hired and paid for the training of a state HIPPY coordinator, who acts as a liaison with HIPPY USA.

Until this year, the Arkansas HIPPY programs were supported primarily by money drawn from the funds allocated to the state under federal Chapter 1 legislation and the Job Training Partnership Act. In 1991, however, the legislature passed the Arkansas Better Chance bill, which, among other things, provided $2.5 million a year in state money to help support HIPPY.

HIPPY	**HIPPY USA**
Southeast Arkansas Education	National Council of Jewish Women
Service Cooperative	53 West 23rd Street
P.O. Box 3507	New York, NY 10010
Monticello, AR 71655	(212) 645-4048
(501) 367-6848	

State Initiatives

State development and financing of family support initiatives is still a relatively new phenomenon. Most activity has taken place within the past six or seven years. Today more than a dozen states are expanding family support initiatives that have grown out of such policy concerns as a desire to prevent child abuse and neglect (Hawaii), reduce long-term welfare dependency (Iowa), prepare children for school (Missouri and Washington State), improve family literacy (Kentucky), and support teen parents (Maryland and Illinois).

State initiatives have tended to emphasize either the development of a network of locally based centers that serve the nearby community, or a home-visiting model that operates out of schools or hospitals and clinics and attempts to reach all families with certain characteristics. Maryland, Illinois, Connecticut, Oregon, and Vermont all chose the family support center model, while Arkansas, Hawaii, Missouri, and the states replicating the Missouri program are among those using a home-visiting approach. What follows is a closer look at one example of each type of state effort: Maryland's center-based Friends of the Family and Missouri's Parents As Teachers home-visiting program.

With statewide expansion, programs face the challenge of modifying their efforts many different ways to fit diverse communities and families. If the state structure in any way inhibits program flexibility, the initiative's effectiveness will be compromised badly. Although the programs in Maryland and Missouri are very different, both states effectively met the challenge of building statewide systems that leave room for local flexibility and responsiveness to the needs of individual families and communities.

Maryland's Friends of the Family Network

Maryland's statewide network of family support centers is administered by Friends of the Family (FOF), an independent agency established with state assistance in 1985 to address the state's high teen pregnancy rates and growing incidence of child abuse and neglect. Today, the public-private entity oversees 13 Family Support Centers throughout the state, which collectively serve more than 1,130 individuals each month. More than 2,400 parents and children received services from November 1990 through September 1991, including almost 900 participants who received in-home services.

FOF's budget, which was $3.2 million in FY 1991, includes contributions from four state departments (Human Resources, Education, Mental Health and Hygiene, and the

Office of Children, Youth and Families) and at least eight foundations and corporations. This budget provides grants of $162,000 annually to the local center sponsors, which include churches, a community college, a housing authority, a school district, a coalition of community groups, and a county agency.

Although the programs vary from community to community, they all primarily target mothers younger than 25 who have children younger than three. All programs provide a range of social support services and assistance in child development, as well as parenting education and assistance to parents completing their GED. The program guidelines emphasize close community ties; inclusion of parents, community leaders, and social service agency representatives on policy advisory boards; direct links with other social services; family strengthening activities; special outreach to hard-to-reach families; and appropriate supplementary services such as child care and transportation.

FOF keeps the local centers informed through its monthly directors' meetings and regular newsletter. It also provides staff training, program assistance and site visits, and helps with fund raising. FOF sometimes takes on special activities, such as a young fathers project funded by Public/Private Ventures to assist young fathers with education, employment, and establishment of paternity. FOF also conducts public education efforts and advocates for family support among public agencies and with the state legislature.

A high-quality, centralized information management system enables FOF to develop reports that describe participants' demographic characteristics, intensity of participation, patterns of attendance, and program impact—information that helps staff members at the local centers manage caseloads more efficiently. The two Friends of the Family centers profiled below have many similarities, but they also demonstrate how programs in the network differ in responding to local community needs.

Family Support Center

The Cecil County center in rural northeast Maryland is sponsored by the Cecil County Community College. Established in 1989 and located in a cinder block building in the middle of a low-rise housing project, the home-like center emphasizes GED preparation or adult basic education courses for teenage parents. With an annual budget of $310,000 and a staff of seven full-time and 11 part-time people, the center can serve about 50 families at any one time, and more than 100 families annually.

Most of the participating families are white and poor, reflecting the population of the area. Many receive AFDC benefits. The average age of the mothers is 19 and most have one child. Mothers typically come to the program after hearing about it from former participants or being referred by health agencies. The young fathers usually are employed in low-paying, low-skilled jobs, and heavy drinking is common. The center's staff members currently are exploring effective ways of reaching out to fathers.

A mother's first few visits to the center are low-key. On the third visit, a staff member conducts an in-depth interview to assess the family's needs and link the family with the appropriate classes and services. Because participants tend to live long distances from the center, drop-in activities are less developed in this program than in urban programs. Participants typically come to the center four days a week for an average of three to six months for scheduled activities. Mothers and children are brought to the center first thing in the morning in the center's van. GED and adult education classes are held in the mornings, and support activities on parenting and life skills such as budgeting and grocery shopping take place after lunch, which is served every day. The county health department offers a regular, free family planning clinic at the center. About half of the mothers stay for the afternoon activities.

In-home services are provided for families with acute problems through two full-time home visitors funded by the state mental health department.

While the mothers attend groups and classes, their children are in high-quality child care run by trained early childhood staff. With assistance from a pediatric nurse practitioner, the staff screens the children for developmental delays and medical problems, making sure the children get whatever treatment is necessary, including immunizations and dental care. The child care workers use the drop-off and pick-up times for informal discussions with the mothers about the children's development.

This combination of structured activities and informal support brings about noticeable changes in both parents and children. The staff members say parents become more patient, using explanation and diversion with their children instead of spanking as they learn more about the needs of young children. None of the center's participating families has been referred to children's protective services.

In their own lives, mothers start taking charge and planning for the future. About half of those who take the GED exam receive diplomas. During the center's first two years, 22 families moved off of AFDC and became self-sufficient. Within the past year, 50 percent of the GED graduates enrolled in job training. Less than 1 percent of the mothers have had a repeat pregnancy while in the program. Prenatal classes are offered for pregnant women, and among the more than 70 babies born to participating mothers only one has been born at low birthweight.

Waverly Family Center

The Waverly Family Center is located in the heart of Baltimore, the state's largest city. The center serves a large, low-income neighborhood in which most of the residents are black and many of the families are headed by single mothers. The adult participants are almost all young, single mothers, many of whom have more than one child. Participants are referred by a variety of helping agencies as well as by friends and relatives. All referrals receive a phone call and many receive a home visit.

The center occupies a small corner house in a neighborhood of dark brick row houses with white-railed front porches. Coming in from the street, a visitor steps right into the child care room for toddlers. Through a small hallway is the infant room, and up the stairs is the kitchen, meeting room, and two tiny offices shared by the staff of 12, most of whom work part time. Although space is limited, the rooms are painted brightly, and the walls are decorated with posters and life-sized stencils of the children who come to the center.

Center programs have evolved over the years in response to needs and interests of the participants. The center opened as a drop-in program in 1985, but the staff found that the lack of continuity that resulted as parents dropped in and out reduced the program's effectiveness. Staff members say the most successful groups are those like the adult basic education class and the teen parents group, for which parents sign up in advance for a series of meetings. The staff also helps with job counseling and job referrals when possible.

Transportation and lunch are provided for all participants. Families needing more intensive services receive visits from a home visitor funded through the Department of Mental Health.

Cindy was a 16-year-old high school student pregnant with twins when she first came to Waverly. Her mother and preschool-age siblings already had been active for some time. Cindy and her mother weren't getting along, and Cindy had moved out of the house. Faced with the prospect of caring for two babies without help, Cindy was a prime candidate for becoming a school dropout. At Waverly she began to attend the group for teenage parents in addition to seeing the counselor.

Counseling helped Cindy and her mother resolve their difficulties. Cindy now lives on her own in subsidized housing with her daughters. She has graduated from high school, but she still attends the twice-weekly teen parents group. Waverly staff members say she is a nurturing parent and her attitude about the future is positive.

Responding to a lack of activities and support for the neighborhood's school-age children, Waverly gradually developed after-school programs for different age groups, as well as a drop-in Homework Club. In addition, individual tutoring is provided by volunteers, who also act as big brothers and big sisters for the children. The youth coordinator often walks around the Waverly area to get acquainted with children who hang out in the neighborhood, inviting them to come to Waverly's after-school programs. Having found that boys stop coming to the center as they approach adolescence, the center hopes to hire a male staff member to work with teenage boys. Waverly also runs a summer camp for neighborhood children at a nearby church.

All of the center's youth activities concentrate on opening up youngsters' horizons, improving school performance, and building self-esteem, with the goal of promoting school success and preventing teen pregnancy later on. The counselor or home visitor visits the families of children who are in need of more intensive services.

The camp and after-school activities bring the center tremendous good will in the neighborhood. Although parents of school-age children usually don't participate in the center except for special events related to their children's activities, several recently joined the adult basic education classes.

With an annual budget of $250,000, Waverly currently serves about 100 parents and 250 children. Its future looks even more dynamic. The AFL-CIO Baltimore Building and Construction Trades Training Council has taken on the center as its community project and is helping to build a new facility across the street from the existing center. With three times more space in the new building, plus the existing building, the center will have room for a greater variety of activities for parents, more child care and adult education programs, and a wider range of programs for school-age children and teens.

Waverly Family Center, Inc.
901 Montpelier Street
Baltimore, MD 21218
(410) 235-0555

Family Support Center
c/o Cecil County Community College
Road B, Hollingsworth Manor
Elkton, MD 21921
(410) 392-9272

Friends of the Family
1001 Eastern Avenue
2nd Floor
Baltimore, MD 21202
(410) 659-7701

Missouri's Parents as Teachers (PAT)

Missouri's Parents as Teachers (PAT) program operates through the public school system. Its goal is to give children the best possible start in life and prepare them for school success by supporting parents in their role as children's first and most important teachers. Started in 1981 in four pilot school districts, PAT became a statewide program by legislative mandate in 1984. Now each of the 543 school districts in the state offers the program. Missouri appropriated $13.1 million to support PAT services during the 1991-1992 school year, when approximately 60,000 families participated.

Most families participate in PAT until their child reaches three and the home visits stop. Parents may participate in other PAT activities, however, until the child enters kindergarten. Families may re-enroll with the birth of another child. The program is designed for families of all education and income levels.

Parents as Teachers has four components: home visits, group meetings for parents, regular monitoring of children's health and developmental status, and referral to social service and other agencies when necessary.

A parent educator visits each participating family at least four times each school year to give parents information about child development and parenting skills along with general encouragement and support. The home curriculum is based on the work of Dr. Burton White and Dr. T. Berry Brazelton, leading experts and advocates in the field of child development. The parent educator answers parents' questions and discusses age-appropriate expectations, helping parents understand their children's behavior and development. At each visit, the parent educator not only gives parents suggestions for games and activities they can do with their children to enhance their development, but also interacts with the child to demonstrate the activities and provide a model for parents. Although parent educators all follow the same curriculum, they are trained to be flexible in the strategies they select to engage parents and communicate the material. Extra visits are offered a family when the parent educator identifies specific conditions of risk.

The parent educator is trained to assess each child periodically for health and developmental problems. When a problem is detected, or when the family needs other kinds of services, the home visitor helps link the family to other agencies.

All PAT programs follow the basic model, although individual school districts modify some elements to better meet local conditions and family needs. The following descriptions draw on information from four Missouri PAT programs:

• New Madrid County School District in rural southeast Missouri, where the population is predominantly white. Four parent educators serve about 500 families at one time in this school district.

• Kansas City School District, which has large black and Latino populations. The program serves about 7,000 families a year and has more than 100 parent educators, 10 area managers, and a central office director.

• St. Louis City School District, which also has a diverse population that includes black families and new immigrant families from Southeast Asia and Central America. In 1991-1992, 35 parent educators worked with approximately 2,500 families of children younger than three, and 16 parent educators provided limited services to another 2,100 families with three- and four-year-old children.

• Springfield Public Schools, which works with a more homogeneous population than those in St. Louis and Kansas City, and has a smaller number of non-English-speaking families. In 1990-1991, 52 parent educators served 5,000 families.

Outreach activities

Because PAT was conceived as a support for all Missouri families, each PAT program has experimented to identify recruitment strategies that are successful in attracting a broad cross-section of participants. In some communities PAT has been perceived as a service for high-risk, low-income families, so specific efforts to recruit middle-class families have been necessary. In other areas such as Springfield, PAT has attracted primarily middle-class families and the challenge has been to interest other segments of the population.

In Springfield, one approach has been to expand beyond the basic services. Like a number of PAT programs, Springfield developed a special program for teen mothers. The program operates in two of the city's high schools, coordinating its efforts with the local Junior League, which funds child care centers in the two schools. Using a special incentive grant from the state Department of Education, the PAT program in Springfield also developed a preschool component, in which children attend preschool while their mothers participate in special parenting classes.

Pat Tennison, director of the Kansas City program, says word of mouth is the most effective recruitment tool among all kinds of families, but the Kansas City School District also uses television and radio to publicize the program and provides speakers for parents' meetings at schools and other community meetings. PAT staff also works closely with local hospitals and state social service agencies for referrals. PAT sends Spanish-speaking recruiters into Latino neighborhoods to talk individually with parents about the program and works with an organization for black males to improve outreach to young black fathers.

In the Kansas City School District, a parent educator works with teens living at a shelter for teenage mothers, holding bimonthly group meetings and private visits. The parent educator reports that it has been difficult to establish rapport with the young mothers, although there have been some recent positive developments. The teen mothers are beginning to refer their friends who have babies. And when the young mothers move out of the shelter, they now leave their new address and phone number with the parent educator so PAT can continue providing support, information, and referrals to other services.

As in Kansas City, parent educators in St. Louis actively recruit at hospitals, clinics, shelters for homeless families, and WIC centers. The program also advertises in grocery stores and other local shops and meeting places. The St. Louis-based food products manufacturer PET, Inc., recently funded a full-time recruiter to assist the parent educators with outreach.

The New Madrid County program, on the other hand, has had to put only a minimal amount of energy into recruitment. In this rural area, PAT generally is well accepted

> "In a Denver developmental screening, a two-year-old child could not build a tower with blocks. I left a set and told the parents to work with the child in a quiet, stress-free situation. When I checked on the next visit he built an eight-block tower and clapped for himself."
>
> A Kansas City parent educator

and little outreach is necessary. More than half of the referrals come from the WIC nutrition program and the rest come from former and current participants.

Immigrant families

In Kansas City and St. Louis, there are large populations of families whose first language is not English, and St. Louis has many new immigrant families from a variety of countries. These families have special needs and pose special challenges for PAT.

In Kansas City, where there is a large Spanish-speaking population, PAT has made it a point to hire bilingual parent educators. PAT materials for parents have been translated into Spanish, and in some areas PAT has begun to offer classes in English as a second language. The language diversity of immigrant families in St. Louis has prompted PAT to work with a local international institute, which provides interpreters to aid communication between parent educators and non-English-speaking families.

Parent educators have found it takes extra time to build trust among immigrant families, so the program has been modified accordingly. Parent educators also say they spend considerable time modeling behavior for parents, and they encourage parents to practice role playing to prepare for potentially stressful situations, such as visits to the doctor.

Intensified services

In Kansas City and St. Louis, where families' needs vary a great deal, parent educators visit more vulnerable families more frequently, scheduling extra appointments and sometimes dropping in spontaneously if they are in the neighborhood. The cities' school desegregation funds augment program budgets for special outreach efforts and extra

Key Questions To Answer When Considering Expansion of Family Support Programs

1. Where will these programs fit within the state's array of preventive programs for children and families?
2. To what extent is collaboration among public agencies and with private agencies part of the overall strategy for expansion?
3. What program components must be retained to assure program integrity and quality, and how will program quality be monitored and ensured as expansion takes place?
4. What has been done to make sure the necessary process and outcome evaluations will be undertaken to measure program effectiveness over time?
5. What structured staff training programs are in place to ensure the initial and ongoing training and supports necessary to maintain quality services?
6. What ongoing sources of funding are available to support expansion?
7. How broad is the constituency for expansion among policy makers, legislators, and agency personnel? Is there community support for expansion?
8. How will this initiative foster improved support for families within state human service agencies?

home visits to families with greater needs. One parent educator in Kansas City reported that a play group was offered twice weekly for isolated families that needed social opportunities for their children. The group continued meeting throughout the summer, with about 10 families attending weekly.

To increase its accessibility, the Kansas City PAT program has collaborated successfully with the city's housing authority to set aside an apartment in each of the city's seven low-income public housing projects for a PAT office, family resource center, and lending library for project residents. The centers are used for group meetings, private family visits, and other activities that are planned jointly by representatives from PAT, the housing authority, and project residents. PAT staffs the centers as necessary.

Group meetings

Several of the school districts have experimented to find ways of encouraging parents to attend the group meetings. School-based PAT programs for teenage parents hold regular meetings on campus immediately after school. In rural New Madrid County, parents' meetings often are held during the day, because most mothers of young children do not work outside of the home. PAT provides child care and transportation for the meetings to make it easier for parents to attend.

The Kansas City and St. Louis programs contract with local cab companies to provide transportation to meetings for families that need it. Small, donated door prizes also are used as incentives for attendance in Kansas City.

How Well is PAT Doing?

When an independent evaluation of the four original PAT pilot programs was released in 1985, the results were very promising. Six years later, an in-depth evaluation of the statewide program suggests that the benefits PAT offers to families have not been diluted by expansion.

In the pilot study, the three-year-olds who had participated in the program since birth were significantly more advanced than a comparison group in language development, problem solving skills and other intellectual abilities, and in demonstrating coping skills and positive relationships with adults.

The children evaluated at the end of first grade also were doing better in school than the comparison group, and their parents were more involved in their education. Teachers also have reported that PAT children are better prepared for school than most other children from similar families.

An independent evaluation of the statewide program released in 1991 shows that PAT has sustained its effectiveness despite the program's broad expansion and the participation of many more traditionally at-risk families. In the new study, the "Second Wave Study of the Parents as Teachers Program," 25 percent of the sampled families had one parent, 16 percent of mothers had not achieved a high school diploma, 22 percent of families received public assistance, and 17 percent represented minority groups. By contrast, less than 10 percent of the original, pilot sample were represented on any of these risk dimensions.

The second wave study did not use comparison groups but evaluated the program's impact on different groups of families by comparing their behavior and characteristics before and after three years of participation in PAT. Although there was concern that services to families might have been reduced as a result of statewide expansion, the evaluation showed that, on average, the latter group of families received 22 home visits during three years, comparable to the 23 visits families received during the demonstration project. There was, however, a substantial decrease in the average number of group meetings attended by PAT parents, particularly minority and single parents. The lower attendance rate generally was attributed to logistical difficulties such as lack of child care or transportation, scheduling conflicts, inconvenient meeting times or locations, and parents' feelings that some meetings repeated material offered during home visits. Minority parents and single parents were most likely never to have attended a group meeting.

Reduced risks. A major objective of the PAT program is the early identification and resolution of potential problems that interfere with learning. The research shows that almost all participating children were screened for hearing and vision problems and developmental delays.

In addition, PAT was shown to be effective in the early identification and resolution of observed risks such as parents' poor coping skills, poor parent-child communication, children's failure to thrive, and children's developmental delays.   Fifty-one percent of the sampled families showed at least one observed risk that parent educators deemed serious enough to impinge on family functioning or the child's well-being. Even among two-parent, non-minority families with mothers having at least a high school education and with incomes above the poverty level—families generally considered to be at low risk—almost half demonstrated at least one observed risk, and fully two-thirds of all child developmental delays were found in these families.

In one-third of the families showing at least one observed risk, the risks were resolved by the completion of the PAT program. And when the risks were parent-child communication and developmental delays, the odds of improving or resolving the risks by completion of the program doubled. More than one-half of the children in the second wave study with observed developmental delays overcame them by age three.

Among families with poor parental coping skills—the most common observed risk —and family stress, the risk was lessened or resolved for half. Generally the family stress that remained unresolved was the result of inadequate income, job-related problems, or the language barriers faced by non-English-speaking families.

Enhanced achievement. In both the pilot program evaluation and the second wave study, children's performance at age three was measured using the K-ABC Achievement Scale, a measure of school-related success, and the Preschool Language Scale. Children in the second wave sample performed significantly higher than national norms on achievement. Among children from families with at least one traditional characteristics of risk— poverty, a mother without a high school diploma, a single parent, or minority status— between 15 and 22 percent scored above the national norm on the achievement scale, and about one-third scored within the average range.

Increased parenting knowledge. Parent knowledge of child development significantly increased for all types of families after three years' participation, except for non-English-speaking mothers without high school education. Non-minority mothers lacking high school education showed the largest gains in parenting knowledge.

Unmet challenges. The second wave study pointed to several unmet challenges in working with families whose first language is not English. Children in these families scored lowest on measures of achievement and social behavior, mothers had low rates of attendance at group meetings, and those without high school education showed the least improvement in knowledge of child development. At this point, researchers who conducted the study say it's impossible to sort out the various ways in which language and cultural differences, program deficiencies, participation barriers, inappropriate evaluation instruments, and other factors combined to produce these results. This uncertainty highlights the need for all family support programs to give rigorous attention not only to designing effective services for families in which English is the second language but also to finding accurate methods of evaluating the results.

The PAT National Center

The PAT National Center was established in 1987 as a cooperative effort of the Department of Education and the University of Missouri-St. Louis to support the program's growth and expansion. The center is responsible for initial and ongoing training of all parent educators. It also provides support services, technical assistance, and supervision for PAT administrators; develops curriculum and program materials; and oversees replication of the program.

Parent educators, who are hired by the local school districts, must have a bachelor's degree or extensive experience working with children and families. Therefore, many are former school teachers, social workers, or child care providers. Before beginning employment, parent educators must complete five days of training, which is available at several state university campuses under the aegis of the National Center. To receive permanent certification, parent educators also must complete annual in-service training for five years.

With the center's leadership, PAT has been replicated in more than 230 sites in 36 states and in Australia and England. Support for PAT programs in the United States comes from a variety of sources, including federal Chapter 1 compensatory education funds for disadvantaged students.

The Honeywell Corp. plant in Albuquerque, New Mexico, has brought PAT into the workplace in partnership with the local school district. And the Bureau of Indian Affairs is experimenting with PAT to help address the problems of underachievement and school dropout among Native American children. The bureau has implemented PAT pilot projects at five sites and plans to expand.

Parents as Teachers
New Madrid County School District
310 U.S. Highway 61
New Madrid, MO 63869
(314) 688-2161

Dept. of Early Childhood Education
St. Louis City School District
5183 Raymond Avenue
St. Louis, MO 63113
(314) 361-5500

Parents as Teachers
Kansas City School District
301 East Armour
Suite 200
Kansas City, MO 64111
(816) 871-6276

Early Childhood Program
Springfield Public Schools
237 South Florence
Springfield, MO 65806
(417) 895-2015

Parents as Teachers National Center
University of Missouri-St. Louis
8001 Natural Bridge
St. Louis, MO 63121-4499
(314) 553-5738

Other Statewide Efforts

Maryland and Missouri are just two of the states that have expanded the capacity of family support programs to reach more children and families. An earlier section of this report describes local programs in Arkansas (page 42) and Hawaii (page 36) that are part of larger state efforts. Kentucky's cross-generation PACE (Parent and Child Education) program and school-reform related initiative to establish family resource centers at or near schools are described briefly on page 59. Among other states with statewide initiatives are the following:

Minnesota has several state initiatives that provide preventive intervention, education, and support for families with children. The Minnesota Early Childhood Family Education Program (ECFE), administered by the Community Education Division of the state Department of Education, sponsors local center-based programs for parents and children up to age five in the vast majority of school districts in the state. Parent discussion groups, parent-child activities, and home visits are among the program components. To complement ECFE, the state also funds a statewide Learning Readiness program, currently limited to four-year-olds and their families, designed to pull health, education, and social services together to offer more intensive comprehensive services for families that need them.

Washington State developed its Even Start program for parents with low literacy skills as a companion to the state's preschool program. Participating parents, who must have a child enrolled in the preschool program, receive literacy training, parenting education, and preparation for job training programs and self-sufficiency. The State Board for Community and Technical Colleges administers the program.

Iowa's Family Development and Self-Sufficiency Demonstration Grant program for AFDC families engaged in welfare-to-work efforts is one of several state initiatives promoting family-centered services. The local demonstration programs use family development specialists and center-based activities to enhance parents' job-related skills, improve family functioning, and foster children's development and school readiness. The local programs are overseen by the Family Development and Self-Sufficiency Council within the Department of Human Services.

Connecticut offers preventive services to strengthen parents' capacity to raise their children through its Parent Education Support Centers. All parents of children 17 and younger are eligible, but priority is given to teenage, first-time, low-income, and minority parents. Centers provide parent education and support services and link parents with other prevention resources in the community. The Division of Program Development at the Department of Children and Youth Services monitors program implementation.

Wisconsin has funded the development of eight Family Resource Centers and intends to fund additional centers in both urban and rural counties. Some centers are housed in schools and hospitals; others are free-standing programs. They all offer both home-based and center-based support services, primarily for new parents and parents of young children. The centers are administered by the Children's Trust Fund, which is run by an independent Child Abuse and Neglect Prevention Board that has funded other parent education programs.

Adding Family Support Activities to Other Programs

Many programs that started with a different focus have incorporated family support into their work. This section describes how a job training program, child care centers, a child care resource and referral agency, a community development project, public schools, an after-school program, and a state department of mental health all have added family support elements. In some instances, the family support approach has been integrated into existing program components; in other cases, parent education or other family support activities have been added to existing services. In all cases, however, implementing the family support philosophy along with activities designed specifically to strengthen and empower families was considered vital to enhancing the effectiveness of the original services.

Cleveland Works:
Helping Parents Combine Work and Family Life

Cleveland Works is a five-year-old job training and employment program in Ohio that has placed 1,200 AFDC recipients, with a total of 3,000 children, into full-time jobs. But Cleveland Works is also much more. Early on, the program's staff realized that it often takes more than a paycheck to put a family on the road to independence and healthy functioning. So Cleveland Works has added family supports and services to its employment training and placement program.

The Family Development Project offers a family education class that trainees may take as part of their regular job training program. The class discusses such topics as family budgeting, child development, parenting skills, and the challenges of raising children as working parents. The project also offers special seminars and activities for parents and families, a full-day Head Start/child care program for children of trainees and program graduates, a summer day camp, and emergency child care services for trainees whose regular arrangements fall though. A newsletter distributed to current and former participants features articles on parenting, health, and child development, along with news of family development activities at Cleveland Works.

Cleveland Works also cooperated with a private health care provider to bring a comprehensive family health center on site. The MetroHealth Downtown Center is open to all county residents regardless of resources. The center staff also offers health education workshops exclusively for Cleveland Works participants on such topics as common childhood illnesses, nutrition and eating habits, and anemia.

Legal problems such as disputes about public assistance benefits, debtor/creditor conflicts, landlord/tenant disputes, and criminal charges and convictions impede employment opportunities for a majority of Cleveland Works' participants. In response, the program established a Legal Services Department in 1989. Job retention rates have risen consistently since then.

When a participant is ready for placement, the program helps weigh employment opportunities against various family concerns. Transportation requirements, location, hours, and availability of child care all are assessed. The program places participants only in jobs that offer full family medical benefits, and staff members assist parents in finding appropriate child care near their homes or jobs. Since the program's beginning in 1986, 85 percent of the graduates have remained employed and off welfare. Follow-up placement and support services are available for former participants who need them.

The program recently inaugurated a special job training and placement program for young economically disadvantaged males at risk of chronic unemployment, many of whom are unmarried fathers. The male participants, their children, and their children's mothers will have access to the program's training and support services, including parent education, Head Start and child care, and family health care.

Cleveland Works
Atrium Office Plaza
668 Euclid Avenue, Suite 800
Cleveland, OH 44114
(216) 589-9675

Parent Services Project:
Child Care and Family Support

The Parent Services Project (PSP), which began in the San Francisco Bay Area, demonstrates the effective expansion of child care centers into family care centers. In breaking a common cycle of parent isolation and stress, PSP helps participating parents nurture their children.

In 1980, eight state-funded child care programs in three Bay Area counties began offering services and support to the families in their programs. Five more Bay Area centers now offer PSP. Families that come to the participating child care centers are black, Asian, and Latino, as well as white. Often they are refugees and immigrant families that do not speak English. Many parents work outside the home and are raising children alone without assistance from other family members. The direct service goals of PSP are to increase parents' sense of self-worth, diminish feelings of isolation, and enhance parenting skills. PSP also helps parents find other support resources available in the community.

The PSP coordinator in each child care program begins by offering families opportunities to socialize, share potluck meals, and enjoy their children together. As parents' trust gradually increases, PSP introduces parenting classes, peer support groups, mental health workshops, and social activities for adults. PSP also offers special groups and activities for fathers. PSP provides respite child care on weekends and emergency child care in the family home if parents need some time alone or to cope with crises.

Quan and Kim Phuong are Vietnamese immigrants who first benefited from PSP's emergency child care and later became involved in broader family support activities. Kim was working in a laundry and Quan was enrolled in a work-training program in appliance repair when one of the couple's three-year-old twins caught a serious flu. The Phuongs took turns staying home to care for him, and by the time he was better, both parents had used up their sick leave. Then the other son fell ill. They knew that if they stayed home with him, Kim would lose her job and Quan his place in the training program.

In desperation, the Phuongs told their children's teacher at the child care center about the problem. She asked the center's PSP worker to arrange for sick-child care at the Phuong's apartment for the week the boy was sick. As a result of this help, both parents began to attend PSP support groups at their child care center, where they have made new friends and are getting help to improve their English.

Because one of PSP's primary goals is to increase parents' sense of control over their own lives, participating parents, with PSP's help, are responsible for deciding what classes, groups, and activities they wish to organize. In addition, two of the major local funders of PSP in the Bay Area established a parent-controlled fund for each program, to be used for family emergencies. Parents have used the fund with great discretion and only after long discussion. At one center, parents tapped into the parent-option fund to help a Southeast Asian family pay for additional child care after the mother was stricken with cancer. Parents in another center used some of the money to buy a new car battery for a financially strapped father so he could get to work.

In 1990 PSP and a large child care program in Broward County, Florida, began working together to replicate the PSP model. As of April 1991, PSP was operating in four Child Care Connection centers in Broward County, serving more than 400 families. By the end of 1991, 30 agencies serving more than 3,000 families in California, Florida, and Georgia had joined PSP. Funding for PSP expansion has come from local school boards, private foundations, corporations, and individuals.

Parent Services Project
199 Porteous Avenue
Fairfax, CA 94930
(415) 454-1811

Bananas:
Resource and Referral and Family Support

Bananas in Oakland, California, is a child care information and referral service as well as a support program for parents in the East San Francisco Bay Area. "If you're 'going bananas' and need information related to children, we're the place to call," reads the Bananas brochure.

Bananas offers parents information about available child care, about other agencies and services that provide help for families, and about child development, health, and safety. Bananas produces flyers on specific topics related to parenting and child development, sponsors workshops, and opens its resource library to interested parents.

Child care referral, one of Bananas' most popular services, includes tips on evaluating services, visiting child care programs, and selecting suitable providers. Bananas serves as a pass-through agency for state assistance funds for infant care for qualified low-income parents.

Bananas has a toy lending library and distributes donated clothing and equipment to needy families. It also organizes dozens of support groups for parents with similar concerns—parents of twins, for example, and parents of children with special needs. For parents who need short-term professional assistance, Bananas has a social worker and a public health nurse on staff. Families that need long-term or intensive services are referred to appropriate agencies. Through the Respite Program, families in crisis can receive subsidies for short-term child care.

Bananas started in the early 1970s with a group of mothers who organized a neighborhood play group for their children. Gradually the group expanded its efforts to help parents find good quality child care. Today Bananas serves 55,600 parents a year with a staff of 18 full- and part-time people.

The families using Bananas' services come from diverse economic, racial, and ethnic backgrounds: white, black, Latino, as well as many new immigrants from Southeast Asia. All of Bananas' printed materials are available in Spanish, Cantonese, and Mandarin, and a Vietnamese outreach worker recently joined the staff. Bananas has prepared a special publication for immigrant families explaining the American child care system.

Bananas
6501 Telegraph Avenue
Oakland, CA 94609
(510) 658-0381

Family Star:
Revitalizing a Neighborhood

The Cole neighborhood in northeast Denver has been plagued by depressed economic conditions, deteriorating housing, drugs, and gangs. Since 1988, however, a community organization called Family Star has been working to strengthen and revitalize the community by empowering residents to take constructive action. Many of Family Star's efforts stress strengthening families and providing a good start for the neighborhood's children.

Family Star grew out of a 1988 meeting of 60 neighborhood residents concerned about a crack house located across the street from a local elementary school. After closing down the house, Family Star purchased and renovated the building and the neighboring houses. Hard work and planning by residents led to Family Star's incorporation as a nonprofit organization, which has been successful in attracting financial support from United Way, the local city council, local businesses, private foundations, and state agencies.

In January 1991 Family Star opened the Infant-Parent Education Center, a Montessori-based child development program, which can serve about 40 neighborhood children younger than three. In preparing for the center, Family Star had provided stipends to a number of neighborhood residents for formal training in the Montessori method. The center now employs four professionals and seven paraprofessionals from the neighborhood. Parents participate in the center's management.

Once a month, the center offers a class in parenting and child development for parents of participating children. Parents are encouraged to come to the meetings as long as their children attend the center. Prenatal and childbirth classes also are offered.

In partnership with the Junior League and United Way, Family Star is planning a new support and counseling program, Cradle of Hope, for 10 pregnant women with drug problems. Family Star President Martha Uriosti says the program hopes to draw a professional case manager from the community to provide counseling support and link mothers with health and social services. Parenting education and support will be provided by staff of the Infant-Parent Education Center. Older women in the community will be recruited to become "cradle partners" to the younger women.

Family Star also is involved in a collaborative project to help community women older than 50 find jobs. The program served 91 women during its first nine months of operation, including two whom Family Star hired as receptionists.

Family Star operates an after-school program at the neighborhood elementary school, which is a public Montessori magnet school. In conjunction with the Denver Community College, Family Star also sponsors adult literacy classes.

Family Star
3305 North Marion Street
Denver, CO 80207
(303) 298-7985

Kentucky Schools:
Family Resource and Youth Service Centers

Kentucky has responded boldly to the 1989 state Supreme Court ruling requiring an overhaul of the state's school finance system. Instead of narrowly addressing the issue of equity in school financing, the state committed itself to reforming every aspect of Kentucky's public education system to improve the education all students receive.

Not surprisingly, discussions of school reform led policy makers to social and economic issues that go far beyond the classroom. Among other things, the reformers considered ways to help families play a more active role in their children's education. As a result, Kentucky's new education system requires a majority of school districts to operate Family Resource Centers for elementary students and their families, and Youth Service Centers for secondary school students.

When fully functioning, the Family Resource Centers are slated to offer access to parenting education, a home-visitor program, child development training, a preschool program, and other activities that respond to local families' needs, as well as referrals to other community services for families.

The Youth Service Centers will provide access to direct services for teenagers, including employment counseling, training, and placement; drug and alcohol abuse counseling; and family and mental health counseling. Some centers also may offer services to teen parents, including parent education classes and child care. In the 1991-1992 school year, the first year of statewide implementation, many centers are emphasizing identification and coordination of existing services and resources, says Hal Fink in the state Cabinet for Human Resources.

The law mandates centers in every school district in which more than 20 percent of the students qualify for the federal school lunch program. Under this criterion, more than 75 percent of Kentucky's 1,300 schools are eligible for centers. In 1991-1992 a total of 133 family and youth centers serving 232 schools were opened. In many rural areas, the family resource and youth service centers have been combined, with one center serving several schools. Some centers are located in school buildings, while others are located in office buildings, storefront offices, or shopping malls. All centers should be operating by the fall of 1996.

Though mandated by the state, the centers are intended to be local programs that respond to local needs. Each center is run by an advisory board, at least one-third of which must be composed of parents. Local teacher representatives, school officials, and business representatives also sit on each board. Two students must be members of every Youth Service Center board. Each board decides on the mix of services its center will offer beyond the mandated core services. The boards may raise additional income to supplement the average $70,000 grant each center receives from the state.

The law requires each Family Resource Center to offer PACE (Parent and Child Education) where the program is available. An innovative state program begun in 1986 and offered through the schools, PACE is designed to reduce adult illiteracy and improve the school readiness of young children. For three days a week throughout the school year, participating parents attend literacy workshops in classrooms neighboring the developmental preschools attended by their three- and four-year-olds. During breaks, parents join their children for play and learning activities. After a lunch provided by the school, parents attend discussion groups on such topics as child development, parenting skills, health, and nutrition, while their children nap. Transportation to and from school is provided.

PACE's aim is to prepare more of Kentucky's citizens for high-skill jobs, improve the state's economy, and end the intergenerational cycle of illiteracy and poverty that plagues much of rural Kentucky. Evaluations of PACE show that participating children arrive at school better prepared to learn and progress at a faster rate than their peers who do not participate. In addition, PACE parents are more involved in their children's education than nonparticipating parents.

**Family Resource and
   Youth Service Centers Branch**
Cabinet For Human Resources
275 East Main Street, 4–C
Frankfort, KY 40621
(502) 564-4986

PACE (Parent and Child Education)
Capital Plaza Towers
500 Metro Street
3rd Floor
Frankfort, KY 40601
(502) 564-3921

Portland Public Schools:
Support for Teen Parents

Since 1986 the public schools in Portland, Oregon, have offered comprehensive services for teenage parents that include important elements of family support because neither schools nor traditional social services alone are well-designed to meet teen parents' needs. As Mary Bromel, co-director of the Portland program points out, teen parents have many issues in their lives, including the competing demands of school, parenting, and growing up. Teen parents need open entry and exit programs that offer flexible scheduling, occasional home tutoring, readily accessible health care and child care services, parenting education, educational and career counseling, job training, and, sometimes, drug and alcohol abuse services for themselves or their partners.

One of the challenges to providing such an array of services, says Bromel, was coordinating the efforts of the school district and the county and state departments of health and social services. It took time, patience, and persistence, she says, to develop habits of collaboration.

The Portland Teen Parent Program is available at 11 sites, three of which offer alternative GED programs and vocational training. One of these alternative programs is a New Chance demonstration project of the Manpower Demonstration Research Corporation.

Some of the teen program sites have day care centers on campus, run by the local Head Start agency, and the project is negotiating to establish more on-site centers. For teen parents at other sites, the Portland project contracts with resource and referral agencies to help parents find subsidized child care. In addition, each of the 11 project sites has a health clinic that provides prenatal care, well-child care, and other basic health services to all students.

Teen parents at the comprehensive high schools attend regular classes as well as a special teen parent class that meets daily. Taught by a school liaison worker, the class curriculum covers such topics as child development, substance abuse, goal-setting, and domestic violence. The class also offers services provided through other community agencies: one day a week a case manager conducts a parent support group; another day a parent educator conducts a hands-on parenting class. The agencies also provide case management, support, and follow-up services for the participants. Counselors work with the young mothers to help them decide on a career or college program.

In the 1990-1991 school year, slightly more than half of the 549 students in the Portland Teen Parents Program received AFDC benefits and were participants in the JOBS program, federally mandated by the Family Support Act of 1988. For the mothers who are returning to school under the JOBS program, the Portland project has a special two- to three-week reentry program called Project Success. A school liaison worker assesses each mother's skills and vocational and career interests to determine whether she would do better in an alternative or a traditional school setting. The liaison worker also identi- fies the support services the mothers need and makes sure they are in place.

Teen Parent Program
Portland Public Schools
531 Southeast 14th Avenue
Portland, OR 97214
(503) 280-5840/ext. 205

Project SPIRIT:
Parent Education Reinforces an After-School Program

Project SPIRIT is designed to boost the self-esteem and academic performance of black students in danger of becoming the next generation of dropouts, delinquents, and teen parents. Developed by the Congress of National Black Churches in Washington, D.C., for implementation by black churches, the project was launched in 1984. Project SPIRIT operates at a total of 32 sites in California, Georgia, and Washington, D.C., and soon will be offered statewide in Indiana. In 1990-1991 a total of 1,400 children participated.

The core of Project SPIRIT is a daily three-hour after-school program for children ages six through 12, during which students receive help with homework and informal instruction to strengthen their basic academic skills. As part of the daily program, stu- dents also participate in activities designed to build life skills and self-esteem.

A second component of the project is a parent education class that uses the STEP (Systematic Training for Effective Parenting) curriculum. Although not every site offers parent education, the Rev. John Borens of the Amos Temple Christian Methodist Episco- pal Church in east Oakland says he believes the parents' class is vital to Project SPIRIT's effectiveness. He recalls observing a grandmother pick up two of the project's brightest children at the end of an afternoon program. "The grandmother wasn't happy about her responsibility, and she called them terrible names as they were going to the car," says Borens. "I realized that if these children go home to a negative situation, it erases the positive messages we give the children. We have to work with the parents as a team so they don't undo what we do."

Yet it's not always easy to convince parents to join the six-week class, says Borens. A volunteer calls to invite every parent or caregiver of the children who attend the after- school program. When parents come to pick up their children or participate in a field trip, the project's staff reminds parents about the class. The church also advertises the class in the community, and the director of the church's child care center urges parents who use the center to attend. At present the class meets twice a week for one hour and is designed to keep parents actively involved through class discussion. Each course takes six weeks to complete, and child care is available.

Loleta Cornelius, a Project SPIRIT staff member, says many parents tell her how much the class helps them understand their children, confessing they didn't realize they could change their children's behavior by changing the way they interact with their children. Mrs. Cornelius says even when a parent doesn't mention the class she often can tell when a parent is attending because the child's behavior improves. Boys who have been disruptive attention-seekers, for example, often calm down and become more patient and cooperative when parents begin giving them more time and attention at home. "Many parents aren't aware how often they tell their children, 'Go away, don't bother me, leave me alone,'" Mrs. Cornelius says. "They don't realize their kids often are acting out just to get their attention. The class makes the parents aware."

Project SPIRIT
Amos Temple Christian Methodist
Episcopal Church
1500 90th Avenue
Oakland, CA 94603
(510) 562-8533

Parents and Children Coping Together (PACCT):
Help for Families of Children with Serious Emotional Disturbances

Thirty local parent support groups in Virginia offer parents of children with serious emotional disturbances both emotional support and concrete help in coping with the challenges of caring for their children. These parents, who often say they feel stigmatized and isolated because of their children's emotional problems, meet regularly in homes, libraries, church basements, and community centers. They share insights and experiences, assist each other with problem solving and decision making, and work to improve their effectiveness as advocates for their children.

The local support group in Pennington Gap in the far southwestern corner of Virginia has been meeting for almost two years. Ten to 12 families gather every month to share information and coping strategies. In the fall, for example, the group held a special back-to-school session for parents and children at which special education procedures were reviewed. The children were organized into "little kids" and "big kids" groups so they could talk about their school experiences and hear advice on coping successfully in the classroom.

The Pennington Gap group and the other 29 support groups operate under the umbrella of a private, nonprofit, parent-run support, education, and advocacy organization in Virginia called Parents and Children Coping Together (PACCT). During the mid-1980s, the Virginia Department of Mental Health, Mental Retardation, and Substance Abuse Services recognized that children with serious emotional problems would not receive maximum benefit from state services unless more was done to support and empower their parents. When Virginia received a grant in 1986 from the federal Child and Adolescent Service System Program (CASSP), which emphasizes the importance of family empowerment to improving services for children with emotional disabilities, the department was able to provide financial and technical assistance to the year-old PACCT organization. The department's goal was to assist PACCT in becoming a genuine resource for parents, while assuring its independence from state government.

Since 1986 CASSP funding and assistance have allowed PACCT to employ two parents part time to direct its work with families. PACCT links parents of children with serious emotional disturbances to support groups in their areas, offers technical assistance and stipends to parents wishing to organize and maintain local groups, and sponsors education and training events. A recent foundation grant will allow PACCT to develop groups for brothers and sisters of children with serious emotional disturbances. PACCT also publishes a regular newsletter, prepared totally by parents, with a circulation that has increased from 200 to 1,500 families, professionals, and advocates in the past five years.

PACCT seeks to reach out to underserved parents, including homeless families in emergency shelters. To increase parent access to support, PACCT offers a toll-free phone number that puts parents in touch with local support groups and needed resources. PACCT also has an office at the Mental Health Association of Virginia, where parents can come just to talk or to get special information. Director Carol Obrochta describes PACCT as a "stigma-free place where families who often are feeling overwhelmed, scared, angry, guilty, and confused can come or call and know they will be able to talk to a parent who understands." Says Obrochta, "It helps to break down that terrible isolation."

Another of PACCT's goals is to make sure parents participate fully in state policy planning and development of services for children with serious emotional disabilities.

Parents and Children Coping Together, Inc.
5001 West Broad Street, Suite 214
Richmond, VA 23230
(804) 285-3636

A CASE STUDY

Support Group Ends Family Isolation

The Allen family in rural Virginia had been suffering silently for years, devastated by the serious emotional problems of their son, Tom, who had been in and out of psychiatric hospitals several times and had become addicted to cocaine as a teenager. Sensing that people were avoiding them, the family felt ashamed to go to church, visit neighbors, or even go to the grocery store. Their pain and grief intensified, however, when at age 16 Tom was arrested as a result of his addiction. At that low point in their lives, the support group for parents of children with emotional disturbances in Pennington Gap, Virginia, became their lifeline.

At group meetings the Allens received help in dealing with the immediate crisis, along with more general support. Drawing from the experience of other parents, the Allens learned how to respond more appropriately to Tom's difficult behavior, how to offer support to their younger child, and where to go for additional help. Most important, however, the Allens finally found other parents who understood their anguish and with whom they could talk openly.

Tom served his time, returned home, and has been drug-free for two years. The Allens believe that Tom was able to improve in part because they finally found help for themselves. Wishing to offer other families the same kind of support and understanding they received, the Allens have convened a PACCT support group in another community for the past three years. One night each week they make a three-hour round trip to help parents there who are suffering and struggling in ways the Allens understand all too well.

What We Know About the Benefits of Family Support

"We have a word of advice for anyone who hopes eventually to expand a model program: Invest in evaluation. Although the temptation to skimp on process and outcome evaluation in order to provide more direct services is ever-present, our advocacy efforts would have been useless without impeccable evaluation data. Our evaluation provided the foundation for our advocacy."

—Gail Breakey and Betsy Pratt of Hawaii's Healthy Start Program,
published in *Zero to Three*, April 1991

Although the research and evaluation base for many of the family support programs described in this report still is being developed, the initial evidence is positive. Evaluations report important benefits for children and families:

- Positive impacts on children's health and physical, emotional, and social development.
- Improvements in parents' knowledge of child development and understanding of how to stimulate their own children's development.
- Improvements in parents' attitudes about childrearing and in parent-child interactions.
- Increases in parents' use of other community resources.
- Reduced likelihood of such negative family outcomes as inadequate prenatal care and unplanned repeat pregnancies, parents' failure to complete school, and child abuse and neglect.

Evidence of program effectiveness comes from many sources: the experiences and observations of those directly involved in family support programs, both as service providers and participants; formal evaluations of specific family support programs; and formal evaluations of early childhood education and development programs that share key characteristics with family support programs.

Reviews of Family Support Research

The growth of the family support movement has been followed carefully and assessed for more than a decade by the Harvard Family Research Project, directed by Dr. Heather Weiss. In a paper prepared for the 1990 Colloquium on Public Policy and Family Support ("Family Support and Evaluation Programs: Evidence from Evaluated Program Experience"), Dr. Weiss and Dr. Robert Halpern, of the Erikson Institute for Advanced Study in Child Development, reviewed 20 research studies of family support programs serving low-income families. Some of the programs stressed school readiness, others focused primarily on health and parenting concerns, and some were designed to meet the special needs of teen parents. All of the reviewed studies had reasonably strong research designs and presented data on outcomes for parents as well as children. Fourteen of the programs were strictly home-visiting programs, two were exclusively center-based, and four offered both types of services.

Weiss and Halpern reported that 13 of the 19 research studies cited short-term improvements in one or more dimensions of maternal behavior, including parent-child interaction, parent responsiveness, and parents' understanding of how to stimulate children's development. Weiss and Halpern also found that many studies reported positive effects on parents' general coping abilities and personal development, although such data were not available for every program.

Studies that reported child outcomes generally documented positive effects on infants' and young children's performance on developmental tests. Weiss and Halpern found, however, that it was difficult to assess the long-term impact on children and families, given the small number of ongoing longitudinal studies. Nonetheless, Weiss and Halpern concluded that "programs that combine parent support and direct developmental services to young children appear to hold the most promise of promoting improved long-term child development outcomes, while not neglecting parents' own developmental and support needs."

The U.S. General Accounting Office (GAO) in 1990 also published a review of evaluations of 72 early intervention programs that used home visitors to offer direct help and link families to other services (*Home Visiting: A Promising Early Intervention Strategy for At-Risk Families*). The review concluded that parents and children participating in home-visiting programs demonstrated improved health and well-being when compared with families not receiving services. Among the specific benefits confirmed by the research were: fewer low-birthweight babies, fewer reported cases of child abuse and neglect, higher rates of childhood immunizations, and more age-appropriate development in children. The GAO noted that program benefits varied depending on the program's goals, target groups, services, and providers. There was insufficient information, the GAO concluded, to support a general assessment of the impact on parents' functioning or on children's long-term functioning.

Among the program evaluations the GAO reviewed was a highly respected study designed by Dr. David Olds and others of the Prenatal/Early Infancy Project in Elmira, New York, specifically to assess the impact of home visiting. The goal of the project, which operated in the late 1970s and early 1980s, was to improve maternal and child functioning and to prevent or reduce the incidence of child abuse and neglect. Trained registered nurses visited families in their homes to provide parent education on promoting good fetal and infant development and to assist the mothers in making decisions about their own education, employment, and future childbearing. The home visitors also identified informal supports available to the women both before and after delivery and linked the mothers with formal health and social services as well.

Four treatment groups were established. Women pregnant for the first time who were teenagers, unmarried, or poor were recruited and randomly assigned to one of the four groups, although any woman in the county pregnant with her first child also could register for the program. Women in all four groups received health and developmental screenings, but only those in two of the groups received home visits. In one group women received home visits up to the time of delivery, and in the other group the women were visited throughout the pregnancy and until the child turned two.

The evaluation showed that all visited mothers had better pregnancy outcomes and rated higher on measures of maternal caregiving than mothers in the control groups. What's more, the mothers determined to be at highest risk who received home visits were less likely than mothers in the control groups to abuse or neglect their children. The visited mothers also showed increased awareness and greater use of a variety of preventive services, including childbirth education classes and WIC nutrition services. Compared with those in the control groups, the visited mothers were more likely to have pursued education or employment goals and to have planned for future pregnancies. Benefits to children in the highest risk families included improved birthweights and improved intellectual functioning on developmental tests.

Evaluations of Programs Described in this Report

A number of the programs discussed earlier in this report have demonstrated positive results for children and families. Some programs have implemented formal evaluations, sometimes using comparison groups. Others are at much earlier stages of evaluation, but are making important efforts.

Parents as Teachers (PAT). An evaluation of the four PAT pilot programs released in 1985 showed that parents and children both benefited from the program and helped make the case for the statewide adoption of PAT. In 1991 the Second Wave Study—an evaluation of the first three years of the statewide program—revealed that PAT had sustained its effectiveness despite expansion. Parents generally improved their coping skills, their knowledge of child development, and their ability to communicate effectively with their children. Children generally performed significantly above national norms on achievement, and more than half of the children with developmental delays overcame them by age three. (See page 48 for more program information.)

CEDEN. A three-year evaluation of CEDEN's Parent-Child Program showed a positive impact on the health and development of children who had participated in 1984-1985. At 24 months of age, the mental development of children in the program was slightly more advanced than that of children in a comparison group. Participating children also had fewer hospitalizations as they got older, a benefit the researchers attributed in part to the home visitors' emphasis on health education. The program was found to have had a positive effect on parents' methods of discipline and on the safety and general appearance of the home. (See page 28 for more program information.)

Parent Services Project (PSP). A three-year study between 1985 and 1988 showed that participating parents significantly reduced their stress levels and maintained them at lower levels compared with a control group. PSP parents also had higher self-esteem. Their attitudes about childrearing and their interactions with their children improved with participation in the program. (See page 56 for more program information.)

Friends of the Family. A 1988 study of the eight family support centers then in place in Maryland by the Maryland Regional Center for Infants and Young Children confirmed that the centers were achieving their goal of reaching very high-risk families. Overall, the researchers concluded, the programs were contributing to a reduced likelihood of repeat pregnancies, clear educational advances by participating mothers, and enhanced family stability. (See page 44 for more program information.)

MIHOW (Maternal Infant Health Outreach Worker Project). An early evaluation of the nine-year-old project demonstrated an impact on good maternal health care practices during pregnancy and improved infant feeding practices. Another early evaluation confirmed that MIHOW's mothers were more responsive to their children, provided more appropriate play materials, and were more involved in helping their children achieve age-appropriate skills than they had been before participating. More recently, focus groups and in-depth interviews with parents and staff revealed that participants felt they had more hope for the future, more control over their own lives, and greater ability to act as their children's advocates since participating. (See page 34 for more information.)

Ewa Healthy Start Program. An evaluation of the three-year Ewa Healthy Start demonstration documented success both in identifying families at high risk of child abuse or neglect and in preventing abuse and neglect from occurring. Of the 241 at-risk families, child abuse was averted in 100 percent of the cases and child neglect occurred in just four cases. No abuse occurred in 99.5 percent of families identified initially as not at risk and therefore not included in the program. However, among families identified as high risk but not served because resources were lacking, the rate of abuse was three times higher than in the general population.

Outcomes for families in nine Healthy Start/Family Support Services sites across Hawaii are equally positive: abuse and neglect have been averted in 99.7 percent and 99.5 percent of cases, respectively. (See page 36 for more program information.)

Research on Early Childhood Education

Observations of positive outcomes from family support and home-visiting programs are bolstered by earlier research findings on broader early childhood intervention efforts, many of which were designed as research and demonstration programs with an evaluation component built into the original design. Many of these programs combined in-home services and other parent education activities with an early childhood education program for the child and confirmed the positive effects of early intervention on children's academic, social, and emotional development. Although the research generally did not isolate the specific impact of parent education and parent involvement activities on the children's gains, the results did show that some of the most effective early childhood development programs involved parents and family.

Perhaps the best known of these research studies was of the Perry Preschool program, which operated in Ypsilanti, Michigan, during the 1960s. The program provided four- and five-year-olds with a comprehensive center-based preschool experience and sent home visitors to talk weekly with the mothers about child development and parenting issues. Evaluations of the results of these combined services showed that participating children performed better on tests of academic skills, intellectual ability, social skills, and school readiness than children in a control group. The mothers showed significant improvements in their confidence and attitudes about parenting and in the provision of a positive and stimulating home environment for their children.

A follow-up study of the same children at age 19 showed that they were more likely than those in the control group to have graduated from high school or to be employed or enrolled in a postsecondary education program. And they were less likely to have become pregnant or involved with the juvenile justice system.

Like the research on the Perry Preschool program, studies of the Family Development Research Program in Syracuse, New York, and the Yale Child Welfare Research Group program in New Haven, Connecticut, showed long-term benefits for children and families resulting from high-quality, comprehensive early childhood programs that included center-based activities for parents and regular home visits. The children in the Yale study, though a very small number, were found 10 years later to be doing better in school than children in the comparison group. Participating parents were more involved in their children's activities, and were more likely to have delayed subsequent childbearing, to have gone back to school, or to have become self-sufficient than parents in the comparison group.

In the 1970s, a number of Head Start demonstration programs with extensive evaluation components were developed to test the effectiveness of various modifications to the basic Head Start model. These projects included significant parent education and support activities, and their evaluations assessed the specific impact of participation on parents as well as on children.

The Parent-Child Development Centers, for example, served mothers and their children from birth to age three in a home- and center-based program that included parent education and support along with enriched child care. Evaluations of the program showed positive effects on the children and significant gains by the mothers on all measures of maternal behavior after two years in the program. Mothers comforted, instructed, and praised their children more than those in the control group, and were more involved in their children's lives.

Continuing Evaluation

At present, additional studies are under way that should offer more useful data on the characteristics of effective community-based family support programs and their impact on both children and parents. For example, both process and outcome evaluations are being conducted of the 24 Comprehensive Child Development projects funded under the Comprehensive Child Development Act. These federally supported demonstrations, begun in 1989 and 1990, are designed to offer low-income families with newborn children a core set of services and supports for a five-year period. The Harvard Family Research Project currently is assessing a variety of program evaluations to explore the relationships between program comprehensiveness and the types and permanence of gains made by program participants. The project also is analyzing the issues confronted during the implementation of nine comprehensive programs.

These and other research and evaluations will help provide a clearer understanding of the sustained benefits of family support and will reveal more about how specific program components affect specific outcomes for specific groups of children and families. These evaluation efforts, combined with the earlier research and the first-hand experience of family support staff in many diverse programs in different communities, will strengthen our ability to help families do the best possible job of nurturing, supporting, and protecting their children.

"When families are able to create and sustain environments that promote healthy child development, their children are more likely to become competent and caring adults. . . . When families break down, all of society bears the far greater costs. . . ."

— National Commission on Children, *Beyond Rhetoric: A New American Agenda for Children and Families*

Putting Family Support Principles To Work

D iverse as they are, all of the family support programs reviewed in this report build on the same underlying principles identified in the report's first section. In a great variety of ways, family support programs:

1. *Build on families' strengths and treat families with sensitivity and respect.*
   - The Parent Services Project offers parents opportunities to plan social, educational, and support activities to meet the needs they identify as important.
   - CEDEN's home visitors are bilingual and bicultural, so they can work effectively with the Spanish-speaking families they serve.
   - The Portland public schools' program for teenage parents offers participants a choice between completing their education at a traditional high school or in an alternative education program that provides GED and vocational training.

2. *Strengthen the family so it can provide a nurturing environment for children within a supportive community.*
   - The Black Family Parenting Education Project offers evening classes on child development and positive childrearing practices to increase parents' self-confidence and effectiveness as parents.
   - Parents as Teachers uses home visitors to give parents specific guidance and support in filling their role as their children's first teacher.
   - Family Focus Lawndale sends young mothers into the community to help new teenage mothers adjust to the demands of motherhood and to encourage them to stay in school.

3. *Offer flexible assistance with a variety of family needs, so problems can be addressed before they intensify.*
   - The Family Place joins forces with its participating families to provide temporary shelter for homeless families in the neighborhood.
   - Bananas links families with appropriate child care providers and other community services and resources.
   - Hawaii's Healthy Start/Family Support Services program sends paraprofessional home visitors to help high-risk families with newborns cope with whatever family problems are creating stress and jeopardizing the children's healthy development.

4. *Foster healthy child development, often by linking families to community resources.*
   - MIHOW home visitors monitor children for health problems and developmental delays and make sure they get appropriate services.
   - The Waverly Family Center not only provides child care for infants and toddlers, but after-school programs and a summer camp for school-age children.

- Visiting nurses in Rhode Island's Family Outreach Program make sure infants born into high-risk families get the best possible start by visiting the families regularly to help with medical problems, monitor infants' development, and link families with other community services.

Building Family Support Programs That Last

Programs that embody the key principles of family support and offer high-quality services are able to make an important difference in the lives of the individual families they serve. But to survive, expand, and assist increasing numbers of children and families, family

Intensive Family Preservation Services

Family support programs offer services designed to meet families' needs *before* crises develop. Another type of program based on family support principles is proving highly effective in helping families already in crisis. These programs provide intensive help that can assure a child's safety, avert the need to remove the child from the home, and help the family develop new ways of coping with problems. Family preservation services, as they generally are called, are described by Frank Farrow, director of children's services policy at the Center for the Study of Social Policy in Washington, D.C.:

"Perhaps the fastest-growing trend in state-funded family services programs is the development and implementation of intensive family preservation services (IFPS). Intensive family preservation services . . . are short-term, crisis intervention services provided to families identified by child welfare, mental health, juvenile-justice, or special education agencies as at risk of having a child removed from the home.

"Such services exist in several program models, but those being developed on the largest scale are patterned after the Homebuilders program developed by the Behavioral Sciences Institute, Inc., in Washington State. This model provides services that are intensive (one worker serving two families, providing 10 to 15 hours per week of family contact), short-term (averaging four weeks in duration), available to the family 24 hours a day and seven days a week, and flexible in offering a mix of therapy and concrete services.

"Begun in the mid-1980s in pioneering states such as New Jersey and Florida, IFPS is now operating in more than 20 states. Although most such programs are funded through state child welfare services, they are being initiated by an increasing number of state mental health systems and juvenile-justice agencies. A state's development of IFPS typically follows a pattern of initial pilot testing followed by gradual expansion as policy-makers assess its impact.

"The growth of IFPS has occurred in large measure because of its promise to reduce states' out-of-home placement rates and to slow states' budget increases in placement costs. To obtain these results, states must target IFPS to those children who would otherwise be placed outside the home by state agencies. When this is done, IFPS appears to prevent unnecessary placements. When services are not carefully targeted to this population, they may provide much-needed assistance but support programs must establish a secure and lasting place in the life of a community.

Family support programs that work and last over time are those that: respond to the community; remain flexible in responding to families' varying needs; build strong links with other service providers; engage in extensive outreach; provide effective staff training, supervision, and support; secure a stable funding base; assess their program's effectiveness; and learn from the experience of similar program efforts.

Responding to the community

Building a family support program is more like making a salad than cutting out cookies, as the directors of three very different family support programs stressed in the January-

cannot have the desired policy impact. Recent evaluations of IFPS in New Jersey and California portray a reduced impact when services are not carefully directed to children who would otherwise be placed.

"Although many states have implemented IFPS on a small scale, a few are now developing this service in larger volume and statewide. Michigan's experience indicates this service's potential when it is more generally available. Michigan's IFPS program, known as 'Families First,' began in 1987 with an appropriation of $5 million, much of which was transferred from within the State Department of Social Services budget for foster care. The program's purpose was to safeguard children in their own homes and to prevent unnecessary out-of-home placement whenever possible.

"Families First has grown rapidly statewide, with much of this growth in Detroit. State administrators sought to "saturate" Detroit with IFPS in order to reduce that city's high placement rates. Michigan contracts for Families First services from private agencies. As of January 1990, 86 staff were providing Families First services in Detroit.

"Detroits' IFPS programs focus on families with substance-abuse problems, because these families represent the majority of foster-care placements. Families First has shown considerable success with these families. The intensive service allows children to remain in their homes safely, while mothers are motivated to seek treatment. Many families have been relocated to improved housing, often in neighborhoods away from the mother's former drug use.

"Since Families First programs have been in operation in Detroit, the city's out-of-home placement rate has dropped from an average increase of 8 percent per year to less than 3 percent. Statewide, counties without Families First programs have continued to experience placement rates that are twice the rate in counties with Families First programs.

"Michigan's IFPS program is the nation's largest, but other states are expanding this service to achieve the same type of coverage. Missouri, Iowa, Kentucky, Tennessee, and New Mexico are among the states building a statewide IFPS capacity."

Frank Farrow, "Services to Families: The View from the States," in *Families in Society: The Journal of Contemporary Human Services*, May 1991, Family Service America.

February 1991 issue of Children Today (Richard N. Roberts, Gina Barclay McLaughlin, and Laurie Mulvey, "Family Support in the Home: Lessons from Pioneer Programs"). Emphasizing the importance of tailoring each program to meet the unique characteristics of the community and families it serves, these directors recommend involving the community intimately in program development.

The program directors CDF staff interviewed agreed on the importance of community leadership in such efforts. The Family Place in Washington, D.C., for example, had a 10-year track record of helping families in a predominantly Latino neighborhood. But the director and her staff understood that what worked in the Latino community couldn't be transplanted wholesale to another community. So when the Family Place began to explore the idea of creating a family support program in a nearby black neighborhood, it asked black community leaders to take the lead, offering to act as advisers and resources during the planning process. That program, which opened its doors in December 1991, then fit well within that community's structure.

Roberts, McLaughlin, and Mulvey also note that program development takes time. "The process of understanding a community and its needs is a developmental one," they write. "It cannot be rushed." This is especially true, they say, because the goal of family support programs should be to supplement the existing family supports in a community, not supplant them.

Over the course of 18 years, Bananas in Oakland, California, consistently has adapted to the changing cultural and language patterns in the East Bay area. Once a program that served primarily white, middle-class families, Bananas now has a staff representing many ethnic and racial groups and publishes materials in Spanish, Vietnamese, and Cantonese, some of which are written specially to help immigrant families adjust to their new surroundings.

Both CEDEN and Survival Skills started with one family support program, then gradually added other programs to address a broader range of family needs. CEDEN branched out from its original focus on early childhood development, for example, to provide a family learning center, where both parents and children can work on basic skills. Survival Skills' Black Family Parenting Education Program was developed to help parents improve their parenting skills and thus avoid the need for its intensive family support program, which serves parents whose children have been placed in out-of-home care.

Remaining flexible

Successful family support programs are flexible, modifying program elements and methods of delivery in light of experience. For example, the Waverly Center in Baltimore, Maryland, shifted from a drop-in program to a more structured program after early experience showed that parents were likely to get more benefit from greater continuity. And when it became apparent that children in the neighborhood lacked constructive after-school activities, Waverly added those.

Local Parents As Teachers programs in Missouri have expanded services beyond the basic state requirements to meet the needs of the families they serve. Some PAT programs offer services in Spanish as well as English; some offer extra home visits to families with special needs. One local program responded to the scarcity of public transportation by contracting with a taxi company to take parents to and from PAT meetings.

Effective programs meet families' needs as they exist, even when they don't correspond to the staff's preconceived ideas. Roberts, McLaughlin, and Mulvey offer a telling example of that flexibility. The Center for Successful Child Development, based in the Robert Taylor Homes Public Housing Project in South Chicago, found that attendance at the parent drop-in center, originally designed to foster parent-child interaction, was very low. Gradually, the staff came to understand that the parents, isolated in their apartments all day with their children, did not want to go to a social setting and spend the entire time interacting with their children. The staff might have insisted on continuing the program as it was designed, but wisely added activities just for parents, so that both the parents' needs and the original goals of the program could be met.

The Avancé Family Support and Education Program had to adjust its outreach to fathers after it found that the incentive of "self-improvement," which brought Latina mothers to the program, did not attract the men. Fathers liked activities that they and their children could participate in together—scouting activities, kite-making, and sports, for example. Once involved through those activities, fathers were more likely to come to classes and group meetings.

Building strong links with other service providers

Collaboration with other public and private community agencies broadens the range and increases the accessibility of services for families participating in family support programs. In Portland, Oregon, the school system realized it would have to join forces with the health and social services departments to offer teenage parents the services they need, including child care, health services, job training, parenting education, career counseling, and individualized case management. In addition, the Portland program collaborates with the New Chance and federal JOBS programs to enable teenage parents who have dropped out of school to receive job training or continue their education in an alternative setting.

Family Focus Lawndale's programs for teenagers and for teens who are parents link the young people to activities sponsored by the state's pregnancy prevention and teen parent support program, Parents Too Soon.

Maryland's Friends of the Family has arranged to have the state Department of Mental Health provide mental health counselors for its family support programs—a strategy that helps both agencies serve families efficiently. Maryland's Guide Family Support Program links participants with drug problems with Guide's Perinatal Drug Program, and Narcotics and Alcoholics Anonymous. The center offers support to families during treatment and recovery. The Family Place was a WIC nutrition site until recently; Planned Parenthood conducts a regular clinic at the center, and the Red Cross and other community organizations offer regular classes.

In some communities, too, family support centers connect with more intensive family preservation service programs that share common values and offer help to families whose children are at imminent risk of placement in out-of-home care (see box, page 72). In Connecticut, for example, families that have been in intensive family preservation programs are linked to activities offered by the state's parent education and support centers.

Coordinating with existing services integrates family support programs more completely into the community, to the benefit of both the program and the community. As family support staff members link participants with existing community services, they are able to identify the gaps in services that need to be filled and advocate for appropriate policy and program changes. In addition, collaboration between family support programs and traditional social service agencies may help bring about needed changes within the traditional agencies.

Conducting extensive community outreach activities

Because family support programs are voluntary by design, most programs—even those that receive many referrals from other agencies—also develop ongoing recruitment strategies. For example, although most families in CEDEN's Parent-Child Program have been referred by public agencies in recent years, CEDEN may reinstitute the former practice of having home visitors canvass door-to-door because they generally can spot children with developmental delays at an earlier age than the public agencies.

Some programs develop a steady flow of new families through referrals by former participants. In addition, many programs use such strategies as neighborhood walks and home and hospital visits to new mothers to encourage participation. A number of program directors have found that families living in the immediate neighborhood of a family support center can be reluctant to participate. Betsy Krieger, former director of the Waverly Center, says she suspects that the fear of losing their privacy keeps some families away. Family Focus Lawndale found that strong outreach to involve the natural community leaders in the center's activities helped establish the program as an accepted community institution and overcome families' wariness.

The Parenting Center at Children's Hospital in New Orleans reaches out to working parents—including many fathers—through brown bag lunches held throughout the downtown area and in large businesses. In New Madrid County, Missouri, the Parents as Teachers program is located near the WIC office. And in Minneapolis and St. Paul, the churches that offer the Black Family Parenting Education Program publicize the program among their own congregations, but also put up notices in neighborhood stores and businesses to interest others outside their membership.

Family support programs generally do not have eligibility requirements or an application process, yet by virtue of their locations many programs serve primarily low-income families. Programs generally locate in the communities they wish to serve, then make their services available to all interested families in the area. This reduces the likelihood that families will be labeled or stigmatized for participating in the program. This approach also increases the chances of attracting a broader cross-section of the community.

Some programs offer a combination of activities—some that are open to all center participants and others that are more narrowly focused. Both CEDEN and Family Focus Lawndale, for example, provide some publicly funded services with eligibility requirements, yet families that qualify for these programs also may participate freely in other center-sponsored activities.

Providing effective staff training, supervision, and support

The highly personalized and individualized nature of family support services means that competent, committed staffs are critical to their effectiveness. Ongoing training, supervision, and support activities for staff are essential components of a successful program.

For many professionals, the transition from traditional social service agencies to family support programs is a challenging one. While most professionals in the social service world were trained in one discipline, the family support approach requires a multidisciplinary orientation. Moreover, working with families as equal partners who make their own decisions—fundamental to the family support approach—is different from the more paternalistic approach that many professionals have used in previous positions. And for program administrators, the range of skills required to run a successful family support program is very broad. They not only need thorough grounding in the family support philosophy, but also excellent management skills and entrepreneurial abilities.

Programs that employ both professionals and paraprofessionals from the local community face special challenges in maximizing the contributions of each. Staff roles and relationships must be defined clearly, and there must be opportunities for staff members to learn from each other's experience.

In the MIHOW program the two sponsoring agencies work closely with the local project sites to develop an initial training program for the paraprofessional outreach workers. And in Hawaii, the private Family Stress Center, which spearheaded development of the Health Start/Family Support Services program, trains program staff for all sites. As members of the communities in which they work, the outreach workers in both MIHOW and Healthy Start already know a great deal about the kinds of problems facing participating families, so training focuses on building the workers' substantive knowledge and practicing appropriate teaching strategies.

Twice-yearly gatherings of workers from all MIHOW projects provide additional training, and a yearly college course for MIHOW workers is offered in Virginia and West Virginia.

In the HIPPY program in Monticello, Arkansas, the paraprofessionals receive three days of initial training and attend weekly in-service meetings to review the coming week's lesson and watch the coordinators role play the activities. The paraprofessionals also attend statewide HIPPY training meetings.

In the Friends of the Family program in Maryland and the Parents as Teachers program in Missouri, the state provides systematic pre-service and in-service training for all staff. Some independent programs, however, must rely heavily on in-service and on-the-job training.

Working with families in need can drain staff members of emotional reserves, and Roberts, McLaughlin, and Mulvey emphasize that workers need support in addition to training and supervision. They write that "without careful assistance in helping [the home visitors] to understand the limitation of what staff are able to do for and with families given the time and the skill limitations of their positions, serious staff burnout can result."

Families Facing the Future in Pittsburgh, Pennsylvania, hired an outside psychologist to run a weekly support group for its paraprofessional home visitors. The Center for Successful Child Development in the Robert Taylor housing project in South Chicago reduced some of the pressure on the home visitors by using a team approach, in which a professional and a paraprofessional have specific areas of responsibility that are equally important and valued.

Securing a stable funding base

For both state-sponsored and independent programs, sufficient and stable funding remains a problem. The Family Resource Center on Webster Avenue in Rochester, New York, is a well-established 10-year-old family support program with a staff of 15, which has launched two other family support centers. Yet director Carolyn Micklem reports that this highly successful program still is plagued by funding worries. She says foundations typically are more interested in helping new programs get started than in providing continuous support for established programs such as Webster Avenue. And although the United Way has been a steady supporter, competition for United Way money is very keen.

Many program directors say that the quest for adequate funding never ceases and requires a large investment of time and energy from staff. Although some fund-raising activity can be beneficial to a program in that it requires developing stronger links to the community and better self-assessment efforts, program development and management may suffer because the professional staff spends an inordinate amount of time on fund raising. Every Friday night for three years, Bananas' staff volunteered to run a bingo game at its building to raise money for an endowment fund. The activity was very popular and successful, but the staff finally decided the effort was too exhausting and discontinued the bingo evenings.

Some programs draw on a range of federal, state, and local health, education, and child welfare initiatives to support various activities. Programs in states such as Maryland, which have established a public-private entity to offer some financial support and ongoing assistance to local programs, find the certainty of public support extremely helpful. But in some cases public funding—especially when it must be targeted to specific services or groups—creates special challenges for maintaining program flexibility and responsiveness. For example, CEDEN originally depended on local public and private funding to support its Parent-Child Program, targeted to children who either exhibited or were at risk of developmental delay. Now, the Parent-Child Program also is supported by federal funds administered by the Texas Early Childhood Intervention Program. The federal and state money is dependable, but as Texas has implemented the federal law, the funds now cannot be used to treat at-risk children who do not yet exhibit developmental delays. This has meant that CEDEN reluctantly has had to shift emphasis to some degree. Such restrictions make it necessary for programs to weigh priorities carefully when accepting public money.

Assessing program effectiveness

All programs need to assess their efforts regularly, both to make their services more responsive to families' needs and to make a case for increased financial investment in their efforts.

Ideally, provisions for evaluating both process and outcomes should be built into the program design and funding scheme of every program. Yet the nature of community-based family support programs makes them difficult and costly to evaluate. Because the challenges associated with evaluation are considerable, most programs are likely to need expert help in designing and implementing good quality assessments, as well as assistance in bearing the financial costs.

To be useful for program development, evaluation must be qualitative as well as quantitative. For example, qualitative changes in parents' and children's self-perceptions and attitudes about the future can be difficult to measure reliably, yet they often play a key role in future outcomes and must be assessed in order to understand a program's impact. And because interactions between staff members and program participants have a critical bearing on program impact, an assessment must consider the quality of home visits—

including, among other things, the ability of the home visitor to inspire trust and relate well to all members of the family—as well as the number of home visits each family receives.

There are other problems to solve in evaluating family support programs, not the least of which is the danger that paper and pencil tests and pressure to complete forms will detract from the welcoming and nonthreatening atmosphere that family support programs seek to create. Other research challenges result from the flexibility of these programs and the variability and multiplicity of the services they offer, the likelihood that families receive simultaneous services from other agencies, and the undetermined impact of outside family events and family relationships on the specific outcomes the program wishes to assess. All of these factors make it difficult for evaluators to apply a traditional experimental research design to family support programs. Then, too, many of the goals of family support programs, such as better family functioning, more positive parent-child interaction, and greater empowerment of families, transcend the particular services they provide, so relationships between specific variables and these general outcomes may be difficult to establish.

For all these reasons, continuing work is necessary to construct evaluations that take into account the unique characteristics of family support programs. Heather Weiss argues that assessments should pay close attention to the "nitty gritty" of family support programs, including how they develop and implement their program; how they recruit participants; and how they recruit, train, supervise, and motivate staff. She also sees the need for more systematic assessments across existing sites to guide the development of new programs and expansion of existing ones.

(text continued on page 82)

Family Resource Coalition

Through publications, conferences, and consultation, the Family Resource Coalition (FRC) gives a national voice to the emerging family support movement. The coalition promotes communication among more than 2,500 programs, provides training and technical assistance, disseminates information about family resource programs to policy makers, and advocates at all levels of government on issues that affect families.

In 1991 the federal Department of Health and Human Services awarded a three-year grant of $1.2 million to the FRC to establish a National Resource Center for Family Support Programs. Among other activities the national center will create and operate a national clearinghouse of information on family support, develop and disseminate new materials for technical assistance, keep track of new developments and state initiatives in family support, and develop an electronic network to facilitate programs' communication with the national center and each other. For more information contact:

Family Resource Coalition
200 South Michigan Avenue, Suite 1250
Chicago, IL 60604
(312) 341-0900

Five Challenges Facing the Family Support Movement
by Bernice Weissbourd

In communities across the country, family resource and support programs are providing comprehensive services designed to prevent problems and promote family well-being. In state after state, programs and the principles upon which they are based are being integrated into state-level human service systems, schools, child care centers, and medical and mental health agencies. As new programs proliferate and old systems are reorganized, the impact and success of the family support approach depends on the degree to which its salient characteristics are maintained and refined. And that, in turn, depends on other factors such as funding and training.

This is a critical juncture in the development of family resource and support programs and a time for the thoughtful consideration of the challenges inherent in change. There are at least five I consider pivotal:

Challenge 1: *Maintaining the integrity of the family support approach as it is integrated into larger systems and human services programs.*

Essential to family support is building relationships between professionals and parents that are based on a sense of trust, flexibility, and shared decision making. The transition to an involved, "family-friendly" approach is likely to be difficult for agency personnel who have related to their constituencies in more distant and formal ways and who are accustomed to the constraints of complex and time-consuming monitoring and reporting systems.

State administrators attempting to change the direction of services report that transforming a system proceeds more smoothly when the lead agency is committed to family support principles and when there are collaborative relationships among staff that reflect those principles.

Challenge 2: *Training professionals and paraprofessionals for positions in family support programs and in existing systems that adopt family support principles.*

There is a danger that the interest in starting programs may exceed the capacity to operate them effectively. It will be necessary to identify the characteristics of high-quality programs, define staff qualifications, and formulate curricula for training.

Although there is general agreement that the training programs themselves should model the principles upon which family support programs function, continued work is necessary to answer some vital training questions: What do practitioners, policy makers, and social service personnel need to know to be effective in their respective roles? What should the training content be? What skills must be learned and what are the most appropriate strategies for transmitting such skills?

If program personnel are not qualified, positive outcomes for children and families are jeopardized. Legislation and planning for family support initiatives and expansion must adequately support pre-service and in-service training.

Challenge 3: *Increase understanding of how communities function and use that knowledge to guide the establishment and operation of family support programs.*

Family support programs are integrated into the community at many levels and in many dimensions, so policy makers must be informed about the multiple ways in which community values and norms influence both political life and family life. The effect of a program on its community, and conversely, of the community on the program, must be explored and understood. More study is needed of the particular elements that impact program-community interaction, so program staff at all levels can work with communities effectively.

Challenge 4: *Refine and expand research and evaluation of family support programs.*

Results of evaluations conducted thus far show that providing social support to parents is associated with positive parent-child interaction, healthier child development and increased education and employability among parents. But there is much more to know about program effectiveness: How can services be better individualized to respond to specific family needs? What program elements are most essential for different target populations? What program structures best accommodate families whose problems range from everyday issues to serious maladjustment? Increased evaluation efforts are necessary to maintain and sustain the support of those who initiate programs and to garner the support of those wary of new approaches.

Challenge 5: *Secure a stable funding base for initiating, maintaining, and expanding programs.*

The private sector alone cannot maintain a system of community-based family support programs, yet budgetary constraints make the competition for public funds intense. Fortunately, the family support approach increasingly is piquing the interest of legislators looking for cost-effective prevention initiatives to reduce future expenditures for treatment and rehabilitation.

Public-private partnerships to fund family support programs have been used with good results in many states. Other states have established new appropriations for family support, or have consolidated categorical funds from existing public funding streams to support new programs. Some states have redeployed funds from existing programs to fund pilot family support programs.

Legislation must be passed that will directly increase the capacity of states and localities to initiate and maintain community-based family resource and support programs. It also is important that funding for family resource initiatives be included in child care, welfare reform, and preschool education legislation.

Meeting these challenges moves us closer to a time when community-based family support programs can be available to families regardless of economic status, race, ethnicity, ability, or disability. When that happens, our nation will have moved from a deficit model focused on preventing problems to a positive commitment to promoting health by providing good beginnings and continuing support to all children and their families.

Bernice Weissbourd is founder and president of Family Focus, a private agency providing comprehensive community-based family support programs in six Illinois communities. She also was active in the creation of the Family Resource Coalition in 1981. She adapted this discussion from her chapter titled "Family Resource and Support Programs: Changes and Challenges in Human Services," in *Families as Nurturing Systems: Support Across the Life Span*, The Haworth Press, 1991.

(continued from page 79)

Family support programs soon will have a new source of help in meeting the challenges of program evaluation through the National Resource Center for Family Support Programs operated by the Family Resource Coalition. The center will provide, among other things, expert assistance in program assessment and evaluation and serve as a national clearinghouse to enhance the flow of information among individual programs and statewide initiatives (see box, page 79).

Learning from other programs

Just as parents and staff need encouragement and support, so do programs. Maryland's Friends of the Family, Missouri's Parents as Teachers, and the Family Focus network in Illinois all provide a formal framework to support local programs. Through common training programs, directors' meetings, newsletters, and other mechanisms, local program staff members have opportunities to share experiences and learn from each other. National networks of program providers, such as the Family Resource Coalition, HIPPY USA, and Parents as Teachers National Center (see Appendix, page 91), also offer helpful support to local programs. The National Committee for Prevention of Child Abuse, in partnership with Ronald McDonald Children's Charities, recently has established the Healthy Families America Initiative to offer technical assistance and support to states and communities replicating Hawaii's Healthy Start/Family Support Program.

Incorporating Family Support Principles into Human Service Systems

Meeting the challenge of strengthening families requires much more than strong networks of family support programs, although they have a vital role to play. It is equally important to improve the effectiveness of traditional human services by incorporating family support principles into the policy and service responses of every state and community agency serving families and children. The strong link between child and family well-being means that existing child-serving systems cannot do their jobs adequately if they continue to focus narrowly on the child, remain insensitive to families' cultural, racial, and ethnic differences, and fail to offer families the supports they need before crises occur.

Serving families well will require changes in relationships among federal, state, and local governments, since federal and state policies and program structures too often hinder local agencies trying to respond comprehensively and supportively to families in particular communities. Public funding streams will need to be realigned so that families' multiple and interrelated needs can be addressed in an integrated manner. And those who work with children and families within agencies must be trained and supported to recognize families' strengths, consider the needs of parents and their children as an interrelated whole, and deliver responsive, individualized services.

System change can begin with small steps. A state might require agencies to propose specific budget initiatives that will make their services more appropriate for families. A social services agency could open up its assessment process to allow families to express their whole range of needs, and its workers could be given the flexibility to collaborate with other public and community agencies to find services to meet those needs. Program eligibility requirements might be modified to ensure that families entering one system could receive appropriate complementary supports from other agencies. And states could pool multiple funding streams to create home visiting programs or to increase the availability of comprehensive service.

In some states, the child welfare and child mental health systems already are collaborating to offer enhanced and early supports to families before problems escalate, or to offer intensive family preservation services to families at risk of having their children placed in out-of-home care (see box, page 72). Family preservation services share the values on which family support programs are based and seek to empower parents to overcome crises and nurture and protect their children.

Some of these new efforts are being supported by local and national foundations committed to encouraging and supporting preventive, family-centered service approaches. For example, through its Child Welfare Reform Initiative, the Annie E. Casey Foundation and the Center for the Study of Social Policy are working with the states of Maryland and North Dakota to develop new ways of funding and operating family-based initiatives that ensure cross-system coordination.

The Edna McConnell Clark Foundation has given Missouri, Michigan, and several other states assistance in establishing statewide systems of intensive family preservation services. The foundation sees those initiatives as important levers for creating broader system reforms that will make human service systems more effective. Missouri's departments of social services, education, and mental health collaborated with the statewide advocacy organization Citizens for Missouri's Children to develop a community-based family preservation prototype that has been replicated statewide. The prototype targets families in the child welfare, juvenile justice, and mental health systems and uses uniform program and staff standards, training protocols, and evaluations, as well as a central intake process. Both the Casey and Clark Foundations now are helping the state restructure state services for children and families to make them more responsive to families.

In recent years, several prestigious commissions have highlighted the need for family support efforts and called for action. The American Public Welfare Association's National Commission on Child Welfare and Family Preservation, which included representatives from a variety of public agencies charged with protecting children, proposed a universal system of family support services as the first tier of a three-tier framework to strengthen and preserve families. The first tier, made up of community-based family support programs, would promote family well-being and prevent problems from developing. The second tier, composed of family-focused community services provided by multiple agencies, would assist families already having significant problems to prevent the problems from becoming acute. The third tier would be a child protection system with a strong family preservation component.

A similar three-tiered approach to family services was recommended by the National Commission on Children, a 34-member bipartisan body appointed by the president and congressional leaders. Throughout its 1991 report, *Beyond Rhetoric: A New American Agenda for Children and Families*, the commission referred to families as the "cornerstone of children's development," and urged the nation to adopt policies and legislation aimed at strengthening and supporting families in their childrearing role.

A family support approach also figures prominently in recommendations for reform in the areas of health care, education, and child abuse prevention. For example, the National Commission to Prevent Infant Mortality recommended home-visiting programs as a critical tool to reduce infant mortality and improve the health of pregnant women, new mothers, and their children. The Council of Chief State School Officers, composed of the 50 state superintendents of public instruction, has endorsed family support and education programs as an important element in strategies to assure school success for all children, including children at risk. And the U.S. Advisory Board on Child Abuse and Neglect emphasized in its 1991 report the contribution a universal home-visiting program could make to a national child abuse prevention agenda.

The achievement of family-focused supports and services for children and families is a long-term goal. Progress may be slow, but important incremental gains can be made over time. States, agencies, and communities can and must learn from each other's experiments — the successes as well as setbacks. As we struggle to reform human service systems, success will hinge ultimately on how well we implement basic family support principles.

> "Today people with widely divergent ideologies can meet on the common ground that the family is central, but, to assure that children grow into sturdy adults, the family needs to be buttressed by social institutions, including churches, schools, community agencies—and government."
>
> Lisbeth Schorr, *Within Our Reach: Breaking the Cycle of Disadvantage*

Action Steps

Parents are and should be the most important people in their children's lives. But that doesn't mean they can or should raise their children without any help. All parents need many different kinds of assistance in caring for their children. All parents are able to do a better job when they are supported in their parenting role and have genuine choices regarding the kind of family environment they can provide their children.

If we are to be committed as a nation to the goal of leaving no child behind, we must value and support America's parents. Although many forms of assistance are helpful in maintaining strong families, there is no substitute for sufficient family income and access to health care, child care, and adequate housing. We must all work together for enactment of employment, income, and tax policies that will make jobs available, ensure that they pay a living wage, and offer basic economic security to families. Such policies must include a refundable child tax credit for all families.

In addition, we must work together to see that a national health care policy is adopted that will ensure basic health care for all Americans, including children and their parents. And we must work for policies and programs that increase the supply of affordable housing, so that all children have a safe and stable place to call home.

At the same time, we must embark on a campaign to offer families the extra help they may need early on to cope with the stresses of daily life and avert crises. Every community must have a range of family-based programs, starting with preventive support services for all families, continuing through targeted programs for more vulnerable families, and ending with highly intensive services for families in crisis.

Family support centers and home-visitor programs are critical pieces of the continuum of services that every community must offer families. These programs provide the early support parents need to carry out their parenting responsibilities confidently and offer their children the love, stability, and security that is so critical to their future development.

The challenge of creating networks of family support programs across the country is a big one. It will require the best efforts of many individuals, outside and inside of government, and must involve simultaneous efforts at many levels. We at CDF believe, however, that the challenge must be met. Our children's futures—and therefore the very future of the nation—is at stake.

Community

Each of us needs to reach out to offer new parents and parents who are struggling with the demands of childrearing the help they need to understand and to respond to the needs of their growing children. Informal support groups in neighborhoods, apartment complexes, or public housing projects, or parent education classes offered through local churches or other community organizations will be enough for many parents. These activities can give parents just the boost they need to carry forward with their responsibilities.

We must learn from parents in our communities and neighborhoods about the supports they need to help them with their childrearing responsibilities. Local religious organizations, Head Start centers, child care programs, and other child-serving organizations can conduct such assessments, then pool their findings. These organizations also can help identify and publicize informal efforts in the community that are helping address families' needs for assistance.

Businesses must implement policies and programs responsive to employees' family needs. Programs might include parenting education classes, in-house family counseling, and resource and referral for child care or other social services. An investment in such services not only has a positive impact on the productivity of the current work force but also is an investment in the work force of the future.

Family support programs must be established in local communities across the country. Religious congregations and other community-based organizations or consortia of such organizations should undertake to establish family support centers in their communities. All civic and social organizations can contribute time and human resources to these efforts, and many organizations can invest money as well. Local businesses might help by donating space, equipment, and supplies for a center, or by offering employee expertise on a *pro bono* basis.

Professionals and others in the community should share their skills with family support centers. Health professionals, teachers, and social workers can offer their special talents and knowledge to assist families. Lawyers, accountants, and those with advertising experience can help with administrative responsibilities. Retired public health nurses might help with health screenings for children. Other seniors might serve as mentors for parents or play the role of grandparents to children in a center's child care program.

Local governments should establish family-centered home- visiting programs to help parents of infants and young children meet their children's health and development needs. Such programs may operate as extensions of health, mental health, social service, or education agencies. They also may operate under the auspices of universities, private agencies, or community-based organizations. A city might try, for example, to reach every first-time mother whose child is born at the city hospital. Home visiting can be done by specially trained parents or community members, or by nurses, educators, counselors, social workers, or other professionals. These programs can offer assistance to families directly and also can link them with other human services.

State

States should establish statewide networks of family support programs, including both family support centers and home-visiting programs. State initiatives should begin by ensuring that every family with an infant or young child, and every family in neighborhoods that now lack such resources, has access to a home visitor or a nearby family resource center. In partnership with communities, states should supply funds to permit expansion of local initiatives and underwrite staff training and support, offer technical assistance, and provide assistance with program evaluation. It is critical, however, that this be done in a way that allows local programs to retain flexibility in responding to the particular needs of the communities and families they serve. An independent entity such as Maryland's Friends of the Family can serve as a useful intermediary between community programs and the state.

States should assess systematically the family support initiatives now under way in their states and bring those initiatives together to maximize resources and the impact on families. Family support efforts in a given state might be buried deep within many different bureaucracies: maternal and child health, early intervention, early childhood education, family literacy, child welfare reform, child abuse prevention, and employment and training initiatives. States must raise the visibility of these initiatives, link them up to serve more families more effectively, and make sure they share common principles and have complementary goals. States might choose to consolidate the administration of these initiatives within a single agency or a smaller number of agencies but continue to encourage referrals and support from many sources. In addition, states should coordinate state efforts with local family support initiatives established by religious congregations and other community groups.

States should establish intensive family preservation services for families in crisis, especially those whose children are at imminent risk of placement in out-of-home care through the child welfare, mental health, juvenile justice, or special education systems. States should provide funding to expand the program capacity of pilot efforts already under way in many communities. States also should support the staff training, technical assistance, and program evaluation activities that are necessary to sustain high-quality programs.

These intensive family preservation service programs should be linked to family support centers and home-visiting programs. Families served by family support programs should be referred to more intensive services when appropriate. Family support programs also can offer essential follow-up services to families that have received intensive crisis intervention services.

States should take steps to make all child-serving systems—health, mental health, child care, education, child welfare, and juvenile justice—more responsive to families' needs. To provide comprehensive services weighted toward prevention and greater support to families, states must restructure programs and financing mechanisms, provide new opportunities for cross-system collaboration, reassess links between local communities and state agencies, train agency staff to work with families in new ways, and involve families in the development and implementation of policies and programs. Such changes will require leadership from governors and those charged with managing public systems; it also will require the cooperation and full support of agency staff. Families and others in individual communities must also be committed to such reforms.

Federal

Congress and the president must enact legislation that will guarantee sufficient federal funding over the next five years to enroll all eligible three- and four-year-olds in Head Start and to serve more infants and toddlers in the Head Start Parent-Child Centers. Head Start, which combines parent involvement with education, health, and social services for children, served only 27 percent of eligible children in 1990. Legislation pending in Congress would convert Head Start to a mandatory spending program and would put funding on a fast track to ensure the program's ability to serve all eligible children by the mid-1990s.

In 1992 there were 106 Parent-Child Centers nationwide. Funding should be enhanced to allow a several-fold increase in the number of centers so that more children from birth to age three and their families can participate.

Congress should fund the Family Resource and Support Grant Program to support the eventual establishment of statewide networks of family support programs in every state. The Family Resource and Support Grant Program, enacted in 1990 but not funded by Congress as of FY 1992, authorizes competitive grants to states to develop, expand, and operate statewide networks of local family support programs. The networks will provide the ongoing training and technical assistance that local programs need. The National Commission on Children recommended a first-year federal investment of $370 million to establish and sustain family support programs in every state, with a large portion of that amount to be used for program planning and start-up.

Congress should authorize ensured funding for family preservation services for families whose children are at imminent risk of placement in out-of-home care. Federal funding for preventive services for families in crisis has lagged far behind funding for out-of-home care, which currently is ensured on an open-ended basis for all eligible children in the care of state child welfare agencies. As a first step toward correcting the imbalance, states must be assured of significant federal funding for the development and expansion of intensive family preservation services. Proposals included in the Family Preservation Act (H.R. 3603) and the Child Welfare and Preventive Services Act (S. 4), pending in Congress in mid-1992, represent important steps in this direction.

Congress should act to enable a small number of states to consolidate federal funding currently available for home visiting programs to build state- or region-wide networks of family-centered home-visiting programs. Currently, a variety of federal funding streams support community-based home-visiting programs. These models vary in their goals, scope, sponsoring agency, and eligibility requirements for participants. States should be given the flexibility to pool the funding for these various programs, provided that the funds can be used to extend home-visiting services to more families. Federal oversight also must be maintained to ensure program quality and careful assessment of the outcomes of such initiatives.

Selected Resources

Barthel, J., *For Children's Sake: The Promise of Family Preservation*. New York, NY: Edna McConnell Clark Foundation, 1991. (Available from Office of Communications, Edna McConnell Clark Foundation, 250 Park Avenue, New York, NY 10177-0026.)

Bruner, C., *Thinking Collaboratively: Ten Questions and Answers to Help Policymakers Improve Children's Services*. Washington, DC: Education and Human Services Consortium, Institute for Educational Leadership, 1991. (Available from Institute for Educational Leadership, 1001 Connecticut Avenue, N.W., Suite 310, Washington, DC 20036.)

Colloquium on Public Policy and Family Support, *Helping Families Grow Strong: New Directions for Public Policy*. Washington, DC: Papers from Colloquium sponsored by the Center for the Study of Social Policy, Family Resource Center, the Harvard Family Research Project, and Maryland Friends of the Family, April 1990. (Available from the Family Resource Coalition, 200 South Michigan Avenue, Suite 1520, Chicago, IL 60604.)

Council of Chief State School Officers, *Family Support, Education and Involvement: A Guide for State Action*. Washington, DC: Council of Chief State School Officers, 1989. (Available from Council of Chief State School Officers, One Massachusetts Avenue, N.W., Suite 700, Washington, DC 20001.)

Family Resource Coalition, Goetz, K. (Ed.), *Programs to Strengthen Families: A Resource Guide*. Third Edition. Chicago, IL: Family Resource Coalition, 1992. (Available from the Family Resource Coalition, 200 South Michigan Avenue, Suite 1520, Chicago, IL 60604.)

Family Resource Coalition, *The Family Resource Program Builder: Blueprints for Designing & Operating Programs for Parents*. Chicago, IL: Family Resource Coalition, 1986. (Available from the Family Resource Coalition.)

Fenichel, E.S. and Eggbeer L., *Preparing Practitioners to Work with Infants, Toddlers, and Their Families*. Issues and Recommendations for Policymakers, Parents, Educators and Trainers, and Practitioners (4 issues), 1990. (Available from *Zero to Three*/National Center for Clinical Infant Programs, P.O. Box 96529, Washington, DC 20001.)

Goodson, B.D., Swartz, J.P., and Millsap, M.A., *Working with Families: Promising Programs to Help Parents Support Young Children's Learning*. Executive Summary, and Summary of Findings. Final Report for the U.S. Department of Education, Office of Planning, Budget and Evaluation. Cambridge, MA: Abt Associates, Inc., February 1991. (Available from Abt Research, MS.DOW, 55 Wheeler Street, Cambridge, MA 02138-1168.)

Kagan, S.L., Powell, D.R., Weissbourd, B. and Zigler, E.F., *America's Family Support Programs: Perspectives and Prospects*. New Haven, CT: Yale University Press, 1987.

National Commission on Children, *Beyond Rhetoric: A New American Agenda for Children and Families*. Chapter 9: Strengthening and Supporting Families. Washington, DC: U.S. Government Printing Office,

1991. (Available from National Commission on Children, 111 Eighteenth Street, N.W., Suite 810, Washington, DC 20036.)

National Commission to Prevent Infant Mortality, *Home Visiting: Opening Doors for America's Pregnant Women and Children.* Washington, DC: National Commission to Prevent Infant Mortality, 1989. (Available from National Commission to Prevent Infant Mortality, Switzer Building, Room 2014, 330 C Street, S.W., Washington, D.C. 20201.)

National Task Force on School Readiness, *Caring Communities: Supporting Young Children and Families.* Alexandria, VA.: National Association of State Boards of Education, December 1991. (Available from National Association of State Boards of Education, 1012 Cameron Street, Alexandria, VA 22314.)

Olds, D.L. and Henderson, C.R., Jr., "The Prevention of Maltreatment," in D. Cicchetti and V. Carlson (eds.), *Child Maltreatment: Theory and Research on the Causes and Consequences of Child Abuse and Neglect.* New York, NY: Cambridge University Press, 1989, pp. 722-763.

Schorr, L.B. with Schorr, D., *Within Our Reach: Breaking the Cycle of Disadvantage.* New York, NY: Anchor Press/Doubleday, 1988.

U.S. General Accounting Office, *Home Visiting: A Promising Early Intervention Strategy for At-Risk Families.* Washington, DC: U.S. General Accounting Office, July 1990. (Available from U.S. General Accounting Office, P.O. Box 6015, Gaithersburg, MD 20877.)

Weiss, H.B., *Pioneering States: Innovative Family Support and Education Programs: Connecticut, Kentucky, Maryland, Minnesota, and Missouri.* Cambridge, MA: Harvard Family Research Project, 1992 Second Edition. (Available from Harvard Family Research Project, Attn: Heather Weiss, Longfellow Hall, Appinway, Cambridge, MA 02138.)

Weiss, H.B., *Raising Our Future: Families, Schools, and Communities Joining Together*: A Handbook of Family Support and Education Programs for Parents, Educators, Community Leaders, and Policymakers. Cambridge, MA: Harvard Family Research Project, Forthcoming Spring 1992. (Available from Harvard Family Research Project.)

Weiss, H.B. and Halpern, R., *Community-Based Family Support and Education Programs: Something Old or Something New?* New York, NY: National Center for Children in Poverty, December 1990. (December 1990 revision of a 1988 paper.) (Available from the National Center for Children in Poverty, Columbia University, 154 Haven Avenue, New York, NY 10032.)

Weiss, H.B. and Halpern, R. *The Challenges of Evaluating State Family Support and Education Initiatives: An Education Framework.* Cambridge, MA: Harvard Family Research Project, 1989. (Available from Harvard Family Research Project.)

Weiss, H.B. and Jacobs, F.H., (Eds.). *Evaluating Family Programs.* Hawthorne, NY: Aldine de Gruyter, 1988.

Weiss, H.B., et al. *Innovative Models to Guide Family Support and Education Policy in the 1990's: An Analysis of Four Pioneering State Programs— Connecticut, Maryland, Minnesota, Missouri.* Cambridge, MA: Harvard Family Research Project, 1990. (Available from Harvard Family Research Project.)

Weiss, H.B., et al., *Innovative States: Emerging Family Support and Education Programs: Arkansas, Iowa, Oregon, Vermont, Washington.* Cambridge, MA: Harvard Family Research Project, 1992 Second Edition. (Available from Harvard Family Research Project.)

Programs Mentioned in This Report
Local and State Programs

**Avancé Family Support and
Education Program**
435 South San Dario
San Antonio, TX 78237
(512) 431-6600

Bananas
6501 Telegraph Avenue
Oakland, CA 94609
(510) 658-0381

CEDEN Family Resource Center
1208 East 7th Street
Austin, TX 78702
(512) 477-1130

Children's Trust Fund
110 East Main Street, Room 614
Madison, WI 53703
(608) 266-6871

Cleveland Works
Atrium Office Plaza
668 Euclid Avenue, Suite 800
Cleveland, OH 44114
(216) 589-9675

Early Childhood Family Education Program
Community Education Division
Department of Education
991 Capitol Square Building
550 Cedar Street
St. Paul, MN 55101
(612) 296-8414

Early Childhood Program
Springfield Public Schools
237 South Florence
Springfield, MO 65806
(417) 895-2015

Even Start
P.O. Box 42495
319 Seventh Avenue
Olympia, WA 98504-2495
(206) 664-9402

Ewa Healthy Start Program
91-902 Fort Weaver Road, #P105
Ewa Beach, HI 96706
(808) 689-8371

**Family Development and
Self-Sufficiency Program**
Department of Human Rights
Lucas State Office Building
East 12th and Grand Avenue
Des Moines, IA 50319
(515) 281-3861

Family Focus, Inc.
310 South Peoria Street
Suite 401
Chicago, IL 60607
(312) 421-5200

Family Focus Lawndale
3600 West Odgen Avenue
Chicago, IL 60623
(312) 521-3306

Family Outreach Program
Kent County Visiting Nurse Association
51 Health Lane
Warwick, RI 02886
(401) 737-6050

**Family Resource and Youth Service
Centers Branch**
Cabinet For Human Resources
275 East Main Street, 4-C
Frankfort, KY 40621
(502) 564-4986

Family Star
3305 North Marion Street
Denver, CO 80207
(303) 298-7985

Family Support Center
Road B, Hollingsworth Manor
Elkton, MD 21921
(410) 392-9272

Friends of the Family
1001 Eastern Avenue
2nd Floor
Baltimore, MD 21202
(410) 659-7701

Hawaii Family Stress Center
1833 Kalaaua Avenue, Suite 1001
Honolulu, HI 96815
(808) 947-5700 or (808) 944-9000

HIPPY
Southeast Arkansas Education
  Service Cooperative
P.O. Box 3507
Monticello, AR 71655
(501) 367-6848

MIHOW
Center for Health Services
Station 17, P.O. Box 567-VUH
Nashville, TN 37232-8180
(615) 322-4773

PACE (Parent and Child Education)
Capital Plaza Towers
500 Metro Street, 3rd Floor
Frankfort, KY 40601
(502) 564-3921

**Parents and Children
Coping Together, Inc.**
5001 West Broad Street, Suite 214
Richmond, VA 23230
(804) 285-3636

Parents As Teachers
Kansas City School District
301 East Armour, Suite 200
Kansas City, MO 64111
(816) 871-6276

Parents As Teachers
New Madrid County School District
310 U.S. Highway 61
New Madrid, MO 63869
(314) 688-2161

Parent Education Support Centers
Department of Children and
  Youth Services
170 Sigourney Street
Hartford, CT 06105
(203) 566-2149

Parent Services Project
199 Porteous Avenue
Fairfax, CA 94930
(415) 454-1811

Project SPIRIT
Amos Temple Christian Methodist
  Episcopal Church
1500 90th Avenue
Oakland, CA 94603
(510) 562-8533

St. Louis City School District
Dept. of Early Childhood Education
5183 Raymond Avenue
St. Louis, MO 63113
(314) 361-5500

Survival Skills Institute
1501 Xerxes Avenue North
Minneapolis, MN 55411
(612) 522-6654

Teen Parent Program
Portland Public Schools
531 Southeast 14th Avenue
Portland, OR 97214
(503) 280-5840/ext. 205

The Family Place
3309 16th Street, N.W.
Washington, DC 20010
(202) 265-0149

The New Community Family Place
1312 8th Street, N.W.
Washington, DC 20001
(202) 265-1942

The Parenting Center
Children's Hospital
200 Henry Clay Avenue
New Orleans, LA 70118
(504) 896-9591

Waverly Family Center, Inc.
901 Montpelier Street
Baltimore, MD 21218
(410) 235-0555

National Resources

Family Resource Coalition/National Resource Center for Family Support Programs
200 S. Michigan Avenue, Suite 1520
Chicago, IL 60604
(312) 341-0900

HIPPY USA
National Council of Jewish Women
53 West 23rd Street
New York, NY 10010
(212) 645-4048

National Committee for Prevention of Child Abuse
332 S. Michigan Avenue, Suite 1600
Chicago, IL 60604
(312) 663-3520

(The National Committee, in partnership with Ronald McDonald charities, is assisting states to replicate Hawaii's Healthy Start/Family Support Program.)

Parents As Teachers National Center
University of Missouri-St. Louis
8001 Natural Bridge
St. Louis, MO 63121-4499
(314) 553-5738

HIEBERT LIBRARY

3 6877 00145 5079

Support the Children's Defense Fund

CDF is a private, nonprofit organization supported by foundations, corporate grants, and individuals like yourself. CDF accepts no government funds.

CDF's work for children depends on your support. Please give as generously as you can.

You may use the form below to contribute to CDF. If you are interested in other types of giving, such as planned giving or endowing a scholarship or program area, please call our director of development for more information or note your interest on the form.

DEAR LORD
BE GOOD TO ME
THE SEA IS SO
WIDE AND SO
MY BOAT IS
SO SMALL

❏ **Yes, I want to support CDF's work for children. Enclosed is my check for:**

____ $25 ____ $50 ____ $100 ____ $1,000 _____ Other

❏ **I would like more information about other giving programs.**

NAME _____

ADDRESS _____

CITY _____ STATE _____ ZIP _____

PHONE: (W) (_____) _____ (H) (_____) _____

Please detach this form and mail in an envelope to: CDF Development, 25 E Street N.W., Washington, DC, 20001. Make checks payable to the Children's Defense Fund.

FS92